THE NEW
MINIATURE PINSCHER

by

Sari Brewster Tietjen

First Edition

HOWELL
BOOK HOUSE

Howell Book House
Macmillan Publishing Company
866 Third Avenue, New York, NY 10022
Collier Macmillan Canada, Inc.

Library of Congress Cataloging-in-Publication Data

Tietjen, Sari Brewster.
    The new miniature pinscher.

    1. Miniature Pinschers.   I. Title.
SF429.M56T54   1988   636.7′6   87-35277
ISBN 0-87605-211-1

Macmillan books are available at special discounts for bulk purchases
for sales promotions, premiums, fund-raising, or educational use.
For details, contact:

                Special Sales Director
                Macmillan Publishing Company
                866 Third Avenue
                New York, NY 10022

10 9 8 7 6 5 4 3

Printed in the United States of America

This book is dedicated to two special Min Pin breeders:

WILLIAM KLEINMANNS

and

E.W. TIPTON, JR.

We have all profited from their interest, dedication and concern.

Raider, one of America's "King of Toys," checks out his kingdom.

Contents

Front cover illustration: Ch. Rebel Roc's Casanova von Kurt, owned and bred by E.W. Tipton, Jr. A legend in his own time, "Little Daddy" exerted a tremendous influence on the breed which is still being strongly felt. Owner-handled to a truly glittering record, he is one of the most memorable Toy dogs that has ever lived.

Photo by Peter L. Bloomer, from the painting by Roy Andersen

Back cover illustration: The "King of Toys" in a luxurious setting as befits his station.

Photo by John Ashbey

Min Pins and kids make the world go round. Nicole Towell from Australia poses with a favorite pet.

Acknowledgments

WHEN THE LATE Elsworth S. Howell asked me if I would be interested in writing a new Miniature Pinscher book for Howell Book House, I initially hesitated in my response. Although I have a life-long involvement with toy breeds, I am not a Min Pin breeder. On a trip to England in the 1950s, I had shown one of Julia and Fred Curnow's Min Pins at the Windsor show, which was an introduction to the early English dogs. However, in order to do the Min Pin breed justice with an educational, informative and interesting book, I knew I would need a lot of help. Mr. Howell told me that E.W. Tipton, Jr. had recommended that I write the book. I talked to Tip about the project and when he assured me of his assistance, I told Mr. Howell that I would be delighted to undertake the task.

I have not regretted that response, as Miniature Pinscher breeders overwhelmingly responded to my plea for help. Under the guidance and prodding of Tip and my good friends, Bill and Ruby Kleinmanns, I was quickly flooded with photos, kennel information, questionnaire responses and other data. Tip, Bill and Ruby acted as my sounding boards as I attempted to unravel the Min Pin. When Tip died in May 1987, not only did I lose my valued consultant, but the Min Pin breed lost one of its strongest advocates.

The beautiful cover painting of Tipton's famous Ch. Rebel Roc's Casanova von Kurt—"Little Daddy"—was painted especially for this book by noted artist Roy Andersen, and the back cover portrait was taken by the talented photographer John Ashbey. The two dogs, one a youngster and the other an adult, are owned by Marcia Tucker and Pam Ruggie. The illustrations of the positive and negative breed points were done by talented animal artist Jacqueline Adams.

Roberta Vesley, American Kennel Club librarian, was a wonderful source for information, old photos and other areas of reference. The libraries at Vassar College and the College of William and Mary also provided needed research materials.

The artwork from the collection of the Vatican, Italy, the Museo Correr, Venice, and the Petit Palais, Paris, provided a glimpse of early small dogs. The private collections of Iona Antiques, Richard Hammond, Bill and Ruby Kleinmanns and Ruth Norwood also contributed lovely bronzes, etchings, paintings and other artifacts for this book. The lovely photograph of a beautiful hackney pony belonging to Ken Harris was tracked down through the gracious assistance of a Bedlington Terrier man, David Ramsey.

I was fortunate in having a friend in Germany, William Ledbetter, who relentlessly ferreted German sources and provided me with English translations. Heinz Hoeller, president of the German Pinscher-Schnauzer Klub, Erna Lang, Elfreida Paech, Sybille Klages, Wilhelm and Irmgard Vietze, Egon Grosskathoefer and Angelika Gravellas are some of the German breeders who graciously responded to the quest for assistance with photos, articles and other documents.

Dr. Harry Spira referred my Australian research request to Mike and Helen Towell, who provided me not only with the background data I needed, but also sent me the lovely poem written by fellow Min Pin owner Elizabeth Pohl.

The English information came from Fred Leonard, secretary of the Miniature Pinscher Club, and Molly Sharpe, Scotland, sent early data and information.

Mr. and Mrs. David Ephrat provided an update on Israel, while my Canadian neighbors, Gerona MacCuaig, Mary Bates and Jean Sparks, gave valuable input. Former Canadian and current U.S.

8

resident and fellow judge, Bob Waters, was another source for early history.

The conversation between two prominent American Min Pin breeders, E.W. Tipton, Jr. and Maisie L. Booher (who is now Mrs. Summers), is a terrific insight into the minds of two breeders who played such a vital role in the development of the American Min Pin.

John McNamara and Dr. Buris Boshell are two other old-timers who quickly responded with data, photos and insight. MCPA president David Krogh and his wife, Sharon, sent hours of tapes to review and answered numerous questions. Porter Washington, handler of Ch. Patzie V. Mill-Mass, one of the great dogs of the past, came up with old photos.

Other specific contributions to the text were made by Buddy and Linda Stevens, Judy Fillpot, Kent and Nancy Grusendorf, Al and Dee Stutts, Vickie L. Jones, Frank and Joan Coluccio and Joe Waterman. Sue Hart put me on the track of two veterinarians, Dr. William C. Harris and Dr. Gordon Lawler, who could help with input on docking and trimming.

Miniature Pinscher breeders contributed enough photos and kennel information to make two books. Unfortunately, due to the book's configuration, everything submitted could not be used. Appreciation to this wonderful outpouring of material goes to Pauline Phalen, Vera Halpin Bistrim, Bernard and Wilma Griffith, Bob and Billie Jean Shuler, Betty Moore, Larry and Penny Dewey, Vickie Jones, Amy Putnam, Connie Wick, Pam Truax, Judith White, Caroline Ofenloch, Shawn Brown, Lerae Britain, Hildegard Olin and Joan Huber, to name some of the breeders who responded.

Special thanks to Seymour Weiss and Sean Frawley of Howell Book House for their assistance and support, as well as to my husband and son for their patience and understanding. Last but not least, I must acknowledge the constant presence and company that my own four-footed companions provided every step of the way.

Sari B. Tietjen
Rhinebeck, New York

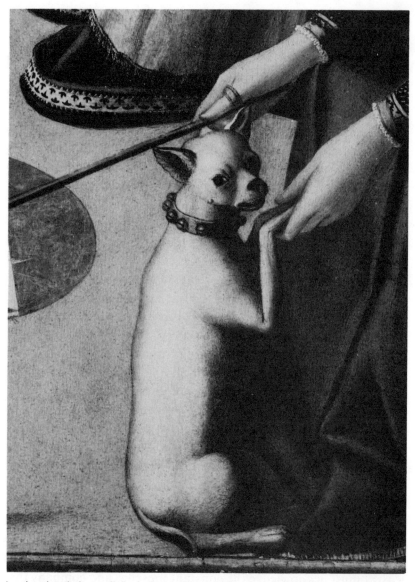

Another detail of a small dog—the pet of two Italian courtesans—who has obvious traits of being an early ancestor of the smooth-haired toy dogs. *Two Courtesans,* 1445–1500, from the collection of Museo Correr, Venice.

Vittore Carpaccio

1

Little Mightiness

THE CHASE

He twitched his nose and sat right up
And flipped his ears on high.
Yet when I asked: "Who are you chap?"
His ears went down like Radar screens
A brightly flashing cotton-tail
Swung swiftly into knee-high greens
And quickly out of sight.

All I could see were stalks of weed
His scent my only guide.
You should have seen my flying start
My leaps to view my quarry.

Oh, holy Hubert have a heart
Come help a poor old Min Pin.
You mighty patron of the chase,
My blood it lusts for mortal sin,
Quick cut the grass and clear my sight
Or better still—just tell that Mug
To stand and have a fight!

Elizabeth Pohl, Australia

THE MINIATURE PINSCHER may be diminutive in stature, but this little dog considers himself to be anything but small. A toy dog with a hearty constitution, curious personality, noble bearing, and affectionate manner, the Min Pin challenges one and all who wish to enter his kingdom on any terms other than his own.

Like many breeds of dogs, the Miniature Pinscher was established through careful crossing of various older breed types. Among the forebearers of the Min Pin is a small dog with a rounded head, upright ears and a smooth coat. This type of dog is visible in paintings dating as early as the 15th century. The Sistine Chapel at the Vatican in Rome features a fresco by Botticelli (1447–1510) entitled *Moses and the Sons of Jethro.* One of the young boys is carrying a small pet dog who has a round head, prick ears and short coat. Another Italian painter, Vittore Carpaccio (1460/5–1523/6), featured a similar dog in his painting entitled *Two Courtesans.* Two beautifully garbed ladies are shown playing with their small pet to relieve the boredom of waiting for customers.

These dwarfish toy dogs were obviously pets of mixed breeding and belonged to a general pinscher type that is known, through the study of canine skeletons and skulls on the Continent, to have existed during the Stone Age. This small dog of basic configuration is no doubt an ancestor of many of our present day similarly configured toy breeds.

2

German Development

THERE IS LITTLE question that the Miniature Pinscher owes its development to breeders in Germany. While the small dog of the 15th century was surely one of its ancestors, the Germans were responsible for crossing it with various canines— including assorted terriers, Dachshunds and Italian Greyhounds— to secure the Min Pin in its present form.

The Miniature Pinscher is part of the larger German Pinscher family, of which the Old German Standard Pinscher is considered by many as the "step-father" of several German dog breeds. As the 1882 engraving of a painting by J. Bungartz, Hamburg, West Germany shows, the most prominent difference between the Old German Standard Pinscher (Glatthaar. deutscher Pinscher) and the Miniature Pinscher (Glatthaar. deutscher Zwergpinscher) was size.

Other than size, the German pinscher family was further segregated by two distinct coat types: wire-haired, or dogs with definite hair length; and smooth-coated, or short-haired animals. When the breeders began attempting to define and separate the varieties, the wire-hairs, such as Schnauzers and Affenpinschers, were no longer supposed to be inbred with the smooth-haired types. Distinctive pinscher breeds began to be seriously established in the mid-1800s.

The word *pinscher* has been the cause of much confusion and, indeed, the breed has not always been referred to as a pinscher. The

Glatthaar. deutscher Zwergpinscher.   Glatthaar. deutscher Pinscher.
(XIII)

A 1882 engraving of a painting by J. Bungartz shows that the main difference between the Old German Standard Pinscher and the Miniature Pinscher was size. Courtesy of the American Kennel Club.

The Old German Standard Pinscher, believed to be the stepfather of all the German Pinscher breeds, almost ceased to exist after World War II, but has since been revived by dedicated German breeders. Pictured is Glenna vom Cronsbach, bred and owned by Egon Grossekathoefer, West Germany.

first German book on dog breeds uses the word *Bentschur* to describe the pinscher and this usage is attributed to local phonetic spelling. This book, *Die Jagd- und andere Hunde in Allen Ihren Verhaeltnissen (The Hunting Dogs and Other Dogs in All Their Relationships)*, was written by Johann Wilhelm Baumeister (1804–46) and published in 1832. Baumeister came from Augsburg or Schwaebisch-Gmuend, Bavaria, which is in the southern part of Germany. It has been surmised by present day German breeders that Baumeister spelled *pinscher* according to the way the word was pronounced in his native Bavarian-German dialect—*Bentschur*. Baumeister believed that the *Bentschur* and the *Pommer* (Pomeranian) or *Spitzer* (larger German Spitz varieties, including the Keeshond) had a common origin. He grouped both breeds together under the category *Haus-oder Bauernhund* (House Dogs and Farmers' Dogs).

In referencing the *Bentschur,* Baumeister wrote:

This breed has the characteristics of liking to be around horses and of hunting wild animals more by means of its keen eye sight than by tracking through scent. . . . The watch instinct of this dog is directed more towards the inanimate belongings and property of his master than towards watching over and caring for his master's sheep flocks or cattle herds. . . . The "Bentschur" has a hostile attitude towards strangers, in whose presence he constantly snarls and growls; he readily distinguishes between his master's friends, however, and beggars or peddlers. He expresses towards the latter an inextinguishable hatred and enmity. . . .

An explanation of the word *pinscher* was offered by Richard Strebel, a noted authority on all German dog breeds, as well as a Miniature Pinscher breeder and judge. Strebel wrote in his book *Die Deutschen Hunde und Ihre Leistung (The German Dog Breeds and Their Achievements)* in 1904–05:

The word "PINSCHER" seems to have been borrowed from the English language. Strangely enough, the English (meaning England) no longer use this word for any of their dog breeds. I consulted, in order to obtain clarity with regard to the etymology of this word, the famous philologist, Dr. Roediger, of the University of Berlin, who is Professor of Germanic Linguistics there. He gave me the following information:

"In the gigantic English dictionary by Muret-Sanders, I find under PINSCHER: dog varieties, smooth-coated English terriers, fox-terriers, the black-and-tan terrier and the wire-haired terriers; also an English dog name such as 'Leo' or 'Bob'; nowadays this name is only used to designate a stingy person, a miser. The verb 'to pinch' can also mean, with regard to a dog, 'to lay hold of, seize, come to grips with, jump at, pounce on or grasp.'

"In Grimm Brothers' *Dictionary of the German Language,* the following is found: 'PINSCHER, PINTSCHER or *Canis gryphus,* a variety of smooth-coated sporting dogs, especially the Affenpinscher and Rat Pinscher, the tail and ears of which are usually cropped during puppyhood, thus the English word PINCH or French: *pincer* to nip off or to pinch off, to clip, trim or crop, thus the name PINSCHER. This explanation can be questioned and doubted because *pinscher* means 'somebody who himself actively pinches,' and not 'somebody who himself is passively pinched.'

"In Henne's *Dictionary of the German Language* can be found, 'PINSCHER—a variety of English sporting-dogs; in the 19th Century borrowed from the English word PINCHER, meaning one who pinches, nips or tweaks.'"

I personally am of the opinion that the dog breed received this name due to its tendency to seize, grasp and hold fast. This name could have just as well been made up by an English-speaking German as by an Englishman.

The early Old German Standard Pinscher was known as a ratter and was kept in barns and stables to keep the rat and mice population at bay. The smaller variety, or Miniature Pinscher, lived in farmers' cottages and performed the same tasks. In the old German book, *Der Hund in seinen Hauptund Nebenrassen,* written in the year 1839 by Professor Dr. Heinrich Gottlieb Ludwig Reichenbach, the smooth-coated pinscher was described thusly:

The smooth-coated Pinscher: *fricatore—vertagus. Vertagus gracilis.* French: Le Basset grele. English: the Pincher. Slender and in all body parts well-proportioned, with narrow, erect ears. Color: primitive wild grey or solid black with reddish markings. The Pinscher is, in spite of its slender body, of robust build and of a steady, cheerful temperament, thus constantly active and alert, without falsehood and deceit. This breed loves warmth and probably likes to stay in the horse stalls for that reason. With its active vivacity, this breed should not be confined during the hunting season. Its hunting instinct is just as pronounced as that of the Dachshund, and if kept inside the house, the Pinscher will always be searching for rats when let out into the backyard; or if he goes into the flower garden, he will always be crouching down in search of moles.

It is most conspicuously obvious how much the Pinscher likes to pounce on, seize and grasp rats, mice and vermin—or even other objects while playing—with his front paws, almost like cats do. A terrier does this in a very different way, much more impulsively, and immediately uses his mouth and teeth.

In his aforementioned book, *Die Deutschen Hunde,* Strebel described a portion of the early breed standard:

In 1880, the first breed standard for the smooth-coated Pinscher varieties was published by the first German Dog Registry. . . . In this standard, the following can be found:

"It should prove to be an extremely difficult task, if not utterly impossible, to determine whether our Pinscher varieties originated in Germany, or whether they are only descendants of the old English Black-and-Tan Terrier, whose old ancestral form was modified or changed by us here in Germany during the course of time. At any rate, our Pinscher varieties are entirely different from the present day Black-and-Tan Manchester Terrier, and our Pinscher has been bred long enough as a constant form here in Germany to justify its being regarded and classified as a German breed."

The question of close relationship with the Manchester Terrier had been previously explored by another noted German animal artist and author, Jean Bungartz, who wrote in 1884, in his *Handbuch zue Buerteilung der Rassen-Reinheit des Hunder (Handbook for Determining a Dog's Pure Breeding)* that "the Pinscher varieties were by no means developed from the English Black-and-Tan Terrier." He stated that since pinscher varieties had always been bred in Southern Germany, the most distant point in Germany from England, he believed that the geographical isolation and distance alone would have made development from English dogs highly improbable. He also maintained that the pinscher breeders of the German province of Wuerttemberg had a much longer pinscher breeding history than did the English breeders of the Black-and-Tan Terrier. He wrote in 1884:

> It cannot be labeled exaggerated, excessive national consciousness if we Germans hold fast and retain the few Pinscher varieties of our fatherland and breed them pure, systematically and with deep understanding. Otherwise, in order to be neutral and unbiased, one would have to reproach the English for having produced during such a relatively short period of time such a large number of different terrier breeds. Had our understanding for and talent in animal breeding—namely in dog breeding—been so pronounced, precocious and widespread as, for example, in England, our German fatherland would, no doubt, have developed from the original Pinscher material surely even more Pinscher varieties.

Regardless of the above statement, there can be little doubt that early etchings and paintings of both the English Black-and-Tan Terrier, or Manchester Terrier, and the German pinschers depict breeds that were similar in appearance, denoting common ancestry somewhere way back in their lines; thus evolved the debate over which came first.

The Germans, who were cognizant of any perceived relationship between the two breeds, took steps to prevent any present day or future intermingling of the breeds. In the 1880 standard, according to Strebel, the color was described as being "shiny black, with yellowish-brown markings; the color of the markings preferably approaches intensive reddish-brown or mahogany; also preferable is a sharp, clear contrast and segregation of these markings from the black basic color, without a sprinkling transition of bronze or yellowish-brown into the black."

This standard went on to further define that "white markings of any description are a major fault, as are black spots within the yellow markings of the legs and paws. (These black spots reveal immediately a crossbreeding of the German Pinscher with the English Black-and-Tan Manchester Terrier.)"

18

Was the Min Pin derived from the Manchester Terrier, the Manchester Terrier from the Min Pin, or did both breeds share a common ancestor? Painting of three Manchesters, circa 1840, unsigned. Collection of Iona Antiques, London.

Painting of three early small dogs, resembling the Min Pin. Unsigned, circa 1870. Collection of Iona Antiques, London.

This Strebel painting, 1901, shows three pinscher varieties: top left, a black-and-rust Min Pin; bottom left, an Affenpinscher; bottom right, a harlequin pinscher—with the long-haired German Silk-Spitz. Courtesy of the American Kennel Club.

In the painting *Mme et M. Mosselman et leurs Filles,* by Alfred de Dreux, three of the white dogs display obvious Min Pin tendencies mixed with hound/terrier crossings. From the collection of Petit Palais, Paris.   *Musees de la Ville de Paris, Spadem*

It is important to note when comparing the two breed standards of that era that it was mandatory for the Manchester Terrier, or Black-and-Tan Terrier, as it was then called, to have "black lines [pencil-marks] up each toe, and a black mark [thumb mark] above the foot" (pencil strips on the toes are permitted in the Min Pin's current American standard, thumb marks are a disqualification).

The 1905 German standard for the Pinscher Dog contained the following:

A truly German breed of dogs which occurs in four types:
1. The smooth-haired pinscher, characterized by a lively, bold carriage and disposition; head and neck carried well up; ears constantly erect and alert; the very short tail stub (these dogs are always docked) curves directly upwards from its base. Of compact body build and standing well up on graceful and rather longish legs; the head somewhat shorter and skull wider and more arched than the English Terrier types. The tips of the ears, which break over, are always cropped to give them a smarter appearance. Eyes are of medium size and of marked attentive expression. Neck is free of pouches or wattles; well-rounded back and neck. Thorax full and deep, more flat than convex laterally. Abdominal underlines rising moderately toward the rear; legs clean-boned and straight from every viewpoint. Toes are well arched and foot round and small. Hair short, close and smooth. Color mostly shiny black with yellowish markings. Less desirable coloring is brown with yellow markings. Still less desirable—solid red or yellow. Regarded as serious defects are weak and too extremely pointed nose; overshot or undershot lower jaw; protruding or bulging eyeball with a tendency to lachrymation; uncropped ears; oversoft hair coating; black spots within yellow markings and any and all white markings;
2. The smooth-haired Miniature Pinscher which, with the exception of size and weight, must meet all of the qualifications of the standard type, but may have slightly shorter and silkier hair than the standard;
3. The long-haired (wire) Pinscher, of standard size, also called "ratcatcher"; and
4. The miniature long-haired (wire) Pinscher.

It was the cross-matings of various types of dogs that formulated the distinctive varieties within the breed. Oftentimes, these

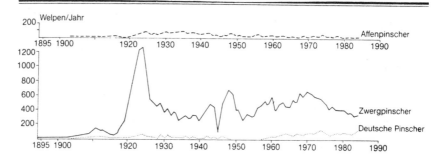

This chart, prepared by Heinz Hoeller, president of the German Pinscher-Schnauzer Klub, tracks the number of Zwergpinscher (Miniature Pinscher) and Deutscher Pinscher (German Standard Pinscher) puppies registered from 1895 through 1985.

P.J. Mene's 1860 bronze of a small, dwarfish dog referred to as "Cropped ear Terrier with a Ball." Collection of Richard Hammond.   *Fox & Cook*

Bronze of a Min Pin dated mid-19th century. From the collection of Richard Hammond.
Fox & Cook

Study of an early Min Pin head. Collection of William and Ruby Kleinmanns.

matings were "hit and miss" affairs with one individual or another deciding to try to change a given type. As previously noted, efforts to devise and secure the pinscher types started around 1850 until the establishment of the first German breed standard, when the mixed breedings ceased to exist. Of the four principal divisions, the rough-haired German pinscher is today's Schnauzer, while many consider the rough-haired dwarf pinscher to be either the present Miniature Schnauzer or the Affenpinscher. The smooth-haired German pinscher is the Old German Pinscher (which, although almost extinct during WWII, is presently being revised in Germany and is very actively supported) and the short-haired dwarf pinscher is our existing Miniature Pinscher.

A painting by Richard Strebel dated around 1901 shows three smaller pinscher varieties standing on steps with two white German Silk-Spitz, an early long-haired breed that is reported to be extinct but closely resembles the Maltese. The Miniature Pinscher is black and rust in color; the Affenpinscher is a black/grey-coated blending; and the Harlequin Pinscher (now extinct) is a tighter rough-coated dog, slightly larger than the Min Pin and smaller than the Old German Pinscher in size. The Harlequin was interesting in that its basic coat color was gray with black spots on the body, but had the usual rust-red markings of the black and rust Miniature Pinschers.

Coat color also played an important part in breed development and separation. The red and stag-red color is said to have come from Dachshund crosses and lead to the term *reh pinscher, reh* being the German word for deer, which the sprightly little red dogs closely resembled. The black and rust color is the original pattern and is believed to have been derived from terrier crosses. Chocolate, a recessive color, was not officially registered as a permitted color in Germany until 1900.

The color white, which has remained taboo since the definitive breeding of Pinschers, is theorized as having come from early terrier/Italian Greyhound crossings. In the early 1800s, it was not unusual to see all-white, smooth-coated terrier/hounds, or white terrier/hounds with black markings, who had positive Pinscher

24

Out all Night, a painting of two Min Pins and four puppies who are obvious housepets. From the collection of Ruth H. Norwood.

A present day German Standard Pinscher—Gibsi vom Cronsbach, bred and owned by Egon Grossekathoefer, West Germany.

features. A painting by French artist Alfred de Dreux (1810–60) of small pinscher-type dogs accompanying their owners on a ride through a park demonstrates two examples of these terrier/hounds. One dog, which is solid white with black points in color, has a pinscher head and body. The other has a white pinscher body with a black-and-white head possessing positive sighthound features.

It has been speculated that the Italian Greyhound cross with the smooth-haired pinscher dogs was devised by the ladies of the more fashionable households who wanted a sleeker, refined, yet sturdy and intelligent pet for their boudoirs and salons. The high-stepping front action of the Italian Greyhound is said to be behind the hackney-like gait requirement for the Miniature Pinscher that exists in the present American breed standard.

In 1900, when the Zwergpinscher was first exhibited at the Stuttgart Dog Show in Germany, Miniature Pinschers were practically unknown outside of that country. Some breeders had ventured to Switzerland in 1882 to exhibit some of their stock, but it was not until the formation of the German Pinscher-Schnauzer-Klub (PSK) in 1895 that a concerted effort began to combine forces with other pinscher breeders and fanciers to promote and secure the different pinscher varieties. PSK, organized within the framework of the *Verband fuer das Deutsche Hundewesen,* or German Association for Dog Breeding, became the registry body for six separate pinscher varieties: Giant Schnauzer, Standard (middle-sized) Schnauzer, Miniature Schnauzer, Old Standard German Pinscher, Miniature Pinscher and German Affenpinscher.

According to a chart prepared by Heinz Hoeller, current president of the German Pinscher-Schnauzer Klub, the Min Pin saw its height of popularity in Germany after World War I until the mid-1920s (approximately 1918–25) when the registration figures for the Zwergpinscher averaged 1,300 each year (present day figures are under 400). Josef Berta, a prominent judge, Min Pin breeder and one of the founding fathers of the PSK, described this period as the "Golden Age" for Min Pins in Germany. In an article he wrote in 1928 for the PSK, he describes the early years of Miniature Pinscher development in Germany:

The Golden Age of the Miniature Pinscher in Germany was the period from 1918 to 1925 when the breed had overcome all obstacles and impediments, all opposition and resistance which had stood in its way during the main period of its development (ca. 1880 until 1918). During this developmental period through which the Miniature Pinscher struggled, clear, sound breed characteristics were selected, captured and locked into all hereditary factors of the Miniature Pinschers. This was a period of enthusiastically active breeders and expert judges, who were absolutely certain of their overall goals and aims, perfectly versed in all aspects of the breed standard. The Miniature Pinscher's noticeable rise in popularity began in the years 1906–07, after the breed standard in the form prescribed by the Pinscher-Klub, after sharp disputes and debates with the Berlin Toy Breed Club, successfully made its way and was supported and upheld.

The first task of the Pinscher-Klub breeders was to convert a poor, weak, frail, tiny lap dog into a healthy, strong, vivaciously sound toy breed. With much patience, composure, stability, consistency and continuity these breeders gradually succeeded in producing and developing a sturdy, sound body framework in a toy breed suited for free, uncomplicated whelping of pups. A great deal of time elapsed until all enthusiasts and breeders of repute were willing to aim for this sturdy, sound body framework in an agile, nimble, athletic toy dog with straight legs, a strong back, well-built hindquarters—typey and full of life.

In the period before our breed standard was adopted and/or universally accepted in Germany, it often occurred that a tiny Miniature Pinscher with a dome-shaped skull, "apple-headed," short neck and devoid of typical Miniature Pinscher expression was placed in the show ring over a sounder, more superior specimen. As a result of our breed standard when progress towards our fundamental prerequisite of a sturdy, sound body framework had become evident, they then worked on getting a harmonious overall dog, including harmonizing the head and neck with body torso and framework. This was the course of the development which led us towards our ideal and eliminated all irregular or abnormal structures and degenerative features, which are still often found in many other toy breeds today. . . .

From 1880 to around 1900, the Miniature Pinscher had merely been a tiny lap dog, usually owned by dignified, aristocratic ladies of higher German society, who did breed their tiny pets with much devotion, but without plans or ideals. . . .

During the years immediately prior to 1925, the goals and breed standard were of top priority in the minds of the highly competent, qualified and certified breed judges, who had watched and contributed to the breed's developmental progress and growth. They all judged with the same evaluation criteria and were absolute experts with regards to all facets of the breed standard. These neutral experts intervened as judges firmly, but objectively and impartially, whenever a fault or deviation from the breed standard was evident.

The early German breeders had managed to stabilize their breed by moving away from tiny, dwarfed animals with apple-shaped heads, bulging eyes and crooked legs. Under the guidance of Josef Berta, the breeders moved toward his vision of what he felt the breed should look like:

I consider as ideal the Miniature Pinscher head which fits with the four-square body, with the strong, upright forequarters, with the sinewy back, with the neck which flows alert and sinewy out of the shoulder and which carries the lines of breeding art; which, as a whole, fits in harmoniously and presents a fitting and aesthetic effect.

I want a whole head and not merely skull with a pair of ugly eyes; I want a head with a well-developed muzzle which works itself strongly out of the skull; and if these two, muzzle and skull, fit together to create a head of beautiful lines, then a uniform and harmonious unity is formed, a perfect picture of the breed is created.

Another view of what transpired in Germany in these early years and an update of the German Min Pin today are presented by Heinz Hoeller, the current president of the Pinscher-Schnauzer Klub:

The first Miniature Pinschers entered in the registry of the German Pinscher-Schnauzer Klub were black with rust-red markings, various shades of lighter red, chocolate with rust-red and one dog that was "salt and pepper" in color. In later years, the darker colors, rust-shaded brownish red and stag red, appeared for the first time.

There were some breeders, not members of the Pinscher-Schnauzer Klub, who wanted to only breed extremely tiny-sized Miniature Pinschers, which had unavoidably led to the production of weak, degenerate tiny lap pets. Josef Berta, on the other hand, wanted

A drop-eared German Standard Pinscher—Finnish Ch. Dorthonion Elisha-Echuir, bred and owned by Minna and Tuija Pajula, Finland.

A red German Min Pin, Ch. Sissy vom Schloss Adolfseck, owned by Philipp Bunk, West Germany.

a Miniature Pinscher with a sound, athletic little body, straight legs, strong back, anatomically correct hindquarters, a nice head/neck line and a complete bite. With this ideal, Berta was always the archenemy of the Toy Dog Club, founded in Berlin, 1902, with whom he was in constant dispute for many years. When he judged a class of Miniature Pinschers, Berta demanded that all the dogs be placed on the ground so that he could examine them with regard to a sound body framework, harmony and correct articulation of body parts, movement and power of locomotion. Up until that time, this procedure for showing toy breeds on the ground had not been customary: toy breeds were always judged at shows in the arms of their exhibitors. It is not surprising that a majority of the earlier Miniature Pinschers produced prior to Josef Berta's intervention had been tiny, frail and weak toy dogs, void of stamina and expressive vigor.

There remained only 814 Miniature Pinschers within the registry after World War I; by 1923, however, the number had climbed back to 3,970. Unfortunately, the large number of pedigreed Miniature Pinschers was deceptive due to the fact that the quality of a vast majority of these dogs had drastically declined. Contrary to the initial period, at which time Berta had not hesitated to place top-quality oversized Miniature Pinschers over inferior ones of correct size, the pendulum by the mid-1920s had swung too far towards diminutive size at the price of less soundness and weaker body substance.

Ernest Kniss of Leipzig, East Germany, who owned the famous "von Klein-Paris" Kennel, wrote the following in the year 1928:

If we had continued to breed with our superior oversized Miniature Pinschers, just as the Miniature Schnauzer breeders have done all these years, I am certain that the present-day Miniature Pinschers would have continued to develop and progress to the same superior plateau in quality conducive to popularity that the Miniature Schnauzers currently enjoy.

Fruendt, owner of the successful kennel "vom Alt-Edelhorst" in Guestrow, Germany, also wrote at that time:

The breeders' passion for extremely diminutive size is always detrimental to and thus dangerous for a breed.

The successful breeder Walter, who specialized in Miniature Pinschers as well as Miniature Schnauzers, wrote in a publication of that era:

A head study of Ch. Ingo von der Pinscherburg, a lovely show dog and delightful pet owned by Wilhelm and Ingeborg Vietz, bred by Erna Lang, West Germany.

Angelika Grabellus' Fredo von den Kleinen Teufeln knows how to enjoy the carefree life of a Min Pin in West Germany.

By all means, the Miniature Pinscher is to remain a toy dog, but also at the same time he must be a sound, sturdy little dog capable of accompanying his master in all weathers.

These experienced, successful breeders had all learned the value of a sturdy, sound toy Pinscher measuring ideally 11 to 11½ inches at the withers. At first, the German Pinscher-Schnauzer Klub did not go along with the wishes of these leading breeders, but in 1936 the upper height limit was raised to 11½ inches. However, no lower height limit was set. This being the case, the Miniature Pinscher breeders were still forced to struggle constantly with the same ever-present difficulties connected with trends which intensified to a craze for extremely diminutive size. . . .

After the bitter decline during and after World War II, the breeding of Miniature Pinschers was again flourishing by the mid-1950s . . . . The breed standard was revised in the year 1956, and the following colors were permitted: (a) black with rust-red markings; (b) all shades of red, including stag red; (c) chocolate with rust-red markings; and (d) blue with rust-red markings. In 1984, the standard was again revised rejecting the chocolate with rust-red markings and the blue with rust-red markings. Isabella was also specifically mentioned as a prohibited color. Presently only (a) black with rust-red markings and (b) all shades of red, except fawn or isabella, are permitted.

In 1956, the upper height limit remained at 11½ inches (30 cm.) while the lower height limit was set at 10 inches (25 cm.), which many breeders still thought too low.

Josef Berta's ideal for the Miniature Pinscher at the turn of the century, which was attained by superior top dogs during the following decades, has remained practically unchanged: an elegant, well-proportioned, sound and sturdy toy Pinscher void of even the slightest signs of degeneration—a tiny utility dog.

Berta got his wish and the Zwergpinscher or Miniature Pinscher breeders of Germany established lines that presented a small, but not tiny; strong, yet not overly muscular; polished, without being too refined, pinscher variety for appreciation by the rest of the dog-loving world.

3

American Development

WHILE MIN PINS have been documented as arriving
in the United States with German immigrants in the early 1900s, it
was not until March 1925 that the first Miniature Pinscher was
registered in the United States with the American Kennel Club. This
dog, a black and rust colored female, was known as Asta von
Sandreuth and received registration #454501 under the breed name
of Pinschers (Toy). Asta was imported from Germany by Mrs. B.
Seyschab of Perry Kennels, Erie, Pennsylvania. The breeder was J.
Bauer, from whom Mrs. Seyschab also imported at least four other
Min Pins at the same time. Two were registered as being wolf-gray
(the old harlequin color), one was pepper and salt (again an extinct
coloration), and the fourth was black and rust. Of the five registered
at that time, four were bitches and one was a male.

As the German dogs increased in popularity in America, the
breeders in this country formed a national breed club. Unlike the
German club, which is a federation of pinscher varieties, the
Miniature Pinscher Club of America, founded in 1929, was solely
dedicated to preserving and protecting the one breed.

Initial entries at dog shows were in the Miscellaneous Class and
the German standard was used as a guideline. With the establish-

ment of a national breed club, the Min Pin was first designated as a member of the Terrier Group, until 1930 when it was reclassified upon petition of the MPCA as a toy breed under the name Pinscher (Miniature). The breed's official name was not changed to Miniature Pinscher until 1972.

The Standard: An Evolution

A study of the evolution of the American Min Pin standard is the best clue to the breed's development in this country. The first standard used by breeders in America during the early 1930s was adopted from a translation of the German version of that period:

General Appearance—From muzzle to stern, trim and clean in outline with well distributed, flexible muscles that must not be knotty or bunchy. Quick in movement, proud in carriage, alert and watchful in manner denoting eagerness and intelligence.

Head—Moderately long and in correct proportion to body and not thick nor cumbersome. Cheeks and lips to be firm and tight and in no way pendulous. Head should have pronounced slope from occiput to muzzle and have appearance of ruggedness rather than too much refinement. Entire head to be well balanced and without distortions. Jaws to be of even length, formed for clean bite, neither overshot nor undershot.

Nose—To be black on the blacks and red-blacks; on the brown and spotted ones the nose may be lighter, flesh colored and spotted nose not to disqualify on the brown and spotted dogs.

Ears—Well set on, pointed and stubby.

Head Faults—Heavy skull, short and snipy muzzle, appleheaded, large or protruding eyes, uneven jaws.

Neck—Strong and muscular, slightly arched and sloping smoothly into shoulders without throatiness or loose skin.

Body—Compact and muscular, length to equal height except in bitches when body may be somewhat longer. Top line to form straight slope from shoulders to hips. Chest to be deep with well sprung ribs; to taper back to clean loin giving free movement to quarters.

Body Faults—Higher at hips than at shoulders, sway back or roach back, low stern, too sloping rump, hollow chest, too wide chest, or too slab sided.

Legs and Feet—Front legs and hind legs to have good bone formations, strong, firm and springy pasterns, toes to be strong, close together, well arched with black toe nails. Well bent stifles with strong, short hock joints and wide, flat quarter muscles. From side view the front and hind legs are to stand at slight angle to body giving appearance of being ready to spring.

Leg Faults—Light bone, weak pasterns, crooked pasterns or hocks, crooked legs, loose shoulders or elbows, cow-hocks or legs bowed out.

Tail—Short and strong, set high on rump pointing upward, cropped short.

Coat—Short and thick lying close to body which must be evenly covered, coat must have healthy, glistening appearance.

Color—A. Bright black, with rusty-red to yellow markings on cheeks, lips, under jaw, a spot over each eye, two spots on chest, also markings on throat, on pasterns, and inside of hind legs and around vent.

B. Solid yellow; solid red; and solid stag-red.

C. Brown; blue or blue-toned with red or yellow markings the same as for A.

D. Spotted on white body, flecked, mostly gray, with black spots and red or yellow markings the same as for A.

Color Faults—White on pasterns, chest, eyebrows or on parts as indicated for A. White markings not to disqualify on D. If yellowish white or grayish white, to be counted as faults on D.

Height—Ideal shoulder height eleven inches, but moderate variations not to disqualify.

The initial truly American standard was not adopted by the Miniature Pinscher Club of America until 1935 and was significantly different from the original German account:

General Appearance—A miniature of the Doberman Pinscher, having on a modified scale most of its physical qualifications and specifications, viz., symmetrical proportions, sturdy though slim, pert, lively, attentive, with well-distributed muscle formation and a carriage suggestive of an active and lively temperament.

General Faults—Heavy set, coarse, poor quarters, too long or short couples, knotty muscles, lethargic, timid or dull.

Head—The head should be in correct proportion to the body.

As viewed from the side—elongated and tapering, with only a slight drop to the muzzle, which should be parallel to the top of the skull.

As viewed from the top—narrow with well fitted but not too prominent foreface.

As viewed from the front—the skull appears flat, tapering forward to the muzzle. Muzzle itself strong rather than fine and delicate and in proportion to the head as a whole; cheeks and lips small, taut and closely adherent to each other. Teeth in perfect alignment and apposition.

Faults—Too big or too small for body, too short or coarse, too long or fine or distorted, top too broad, foreface too prominent, skull too round or hollow with too much stop, poor teeth, jaws undershot or overshot.

Eyes—Full, slightly oval, almost round, clear and bright, dark, even to a true black, set wide apart and fitted well into the sockets.

Faults—Too round and full, too small or large, too bulging or deep-set, too close or far apart.

Ears—Well set, and placed, firm, upstanding (or when legal, cropped short, pointed and upstanding).

Faults—Poorly set, placed low, weak or hanging, or poorly cropped.

Nose—Black in black and tan, red or stag-red.

Faults—Brown or spotted in black and tan, red or stag-red.

Neck—Slightly arched, and gracefully curved, blending into the shoulders, relatively short, muscular, and free from throatiness. Length from occiput to withers equal distance from nose to occiput.

Faults—Too straight, or too curved. Too thick or too thin. Too long or short, knotty muscles, loose flabby or wrinkled skin.

Body—Compact, wedge shaped, muscular with well sprung ribs, the base line of which is level with the points of the elbows; well knit muscular quarters set wide apart, with back level or slightly sloping towards the rear. Length of males equals height, females may be slightly longer.

Faults—Chest too narrow or barrel shaped, quarters too wide or too close to each other, too thin or too fat, sloping rump, swayback, roachback, wryback, hips higher or considerably lower than shoulders.

Legs and Feet—Straight and upstanding as viewed from the front or rear with strong bone development and small joints; viewed from side—all adjacent bones should appear well angulated with well-muscled stifles, short well-developed hocks, well-knit flexible pasterns, strong, well-arched and closely knit toes with thick blunt nails.

Faults—Bow or X-legs—too thick or too thin bone development, large joints, thin stifles, large or crooked hocks, floating knee caps, weak pasterns, spreading flat feet, feet turning in or out.

Tail—Set high, broad, held erect and cropped 1 to 2 inches.

Faults—Set too low, too thin, drooping, hanging or poorly cropped.

Coat—Thick, hard, short, straight, and lustrous, closely adhering to and uniformly covering the body.

Faults—Thin, too short, dull, upstanding, curly, dry, areas of various thickness or bald spots.

Color—1. Lustrous black with tan, rust-red or yellow markings on cheeks, lips, lower jaw, throat, above eyes, twin spots on chest, lower half or forelegs, inside of hind legs and vent region. Black pencil stripes on toes. **Faults**—light colored or white, very dark or sooty spots—in listed markings.

2. Solid yellow.

3. Solid red or stag-red.

4. Solid brown or brown with red or yellow markings.

5. Solid blue or blue toned with red or yellow markings.

Height—Approximately 11½ inches at the shoulder or withers, with a slight variation permissible.

Faults—Too small or too large.

Weight—Five to ten pounds.

Value of Points

General Appearance and Movement	25
Nose	5
Mouth	5
Eyes	5
Ears	5
Neck	5
Body	15
Feet	5
Color	10
Coat	15
Tail	5
Total Number of Points	100

There are several interesting aspects of this first actual American standard. One is the mention of the Doberman Pinscher under General Appearance. The Miniature Pinscher is not a smaller

This Miniature Pinscher likes to play on the belly of his tranquil cousin, the Doberman Pinscher.

This 1946 champion is the heavier style predominant in the breed's early development in America. Courtesy of the American Kennel Club.

variety of the Doberman and never was, yet a national breed club wrote a standard that implies such. The only possible reason for this could be that the early American breeders used this analogy in an attempt to describe an overview of the breed by relating it to a more popular breed of a similar style. While the Min Pin is not a direct descendent of the Doberman (the Min Pin is, in fact, an older breed), it is more likely that the Min Pin and Doberman do share a common ancestor in the Old German Standard Pinscher. All mention of a likeness with the Doberman Pinscher was eliminated from the Min Pin standard in 1950 when the standard was completely revised.

The coat colorations permitted under the 1935 standard reflect the early acceptance of solid yellow and blue, or blue with red or yellow markings, while light colored or white in listed markings is considered a fault. The 1950 revision altered this section to eliminate any reference to solid yellow or blue and made "any color other than listed" a fault. A disqualification was also added in 1950 to eliminate the Manchester Terrier "thumb marks," as well as white on feet or forechest exceeding one-half inch in diameter.

Weight and size requirements have undergone a considerable change over the years. The 1935 standard permitted five to ten pounds in weight and 11½ inches in height—with anything over or under being a fault. According to articles of the day, breeders engaged in a lot of discussions regarding these limitations and their effect on the breed at that time. Various comments were:

> "If we have a variation of five pounds in weight, the height must be approximate."
>
> "It is very hard to get a small dog true to type and sound. This should be recognized by the judges. If we breed too large, the Miniature Pinscher will be coarse, and might again be moved into the Terrier Group."
>
> "Size is a factor we have discussed in the *Kennel Gazette* quite frequently. Still there seems to be a tendency of showing too small dogs with their faults, rather than a good size specimen with better legs and skeleton formation."
>
> "A friend recently told me of asking a breeder of Miniature Pinschers what was the most desirous weight for the breed. He was told that five pounds was the weight, because the public liked small dogs, and it was easier to sell them at that weight."

". . . if we should let the breed become lighter, we will soon find our dogs with certain characteristics which are not faults in the standard. It would not take many years before we would have appleheads and protruding eyes again. Not to mention weak hindquarters and poor skeleton formation generally."

In October 1938, the MPCA, with the approval of the American Kennel Club, made this first change to their standard:

The last paragraph of said Standard entitled "Weight" is changed to read:

Males	6–10 lbs.
Females	6½–10 lbs.

With this alteration early emphasis was placed on weight rather than height. Fear was expressed that tiny dogs would lead to undesirable dwarfish traits. In the full standard revision of 1950, specific height variations were added to the weight restrictions so that the new 1950 standard read:

Size and Weight: Size to range from 10 inches to 12½ inches at the withers, with a preference of 11 inches to 11½ inches, weight to be governed by size and condition ranging from 6–9 lbs. for males and 6½–10 lbs. for females. A squarely built specimen within the size limit, in condition, will conform to weight range. It is recommended that at all dog shows prescribed size and weight will be governed by condition.
Faults: Over-size; under-size, too fat; too lean.

The disqualification for size was not adopted by the national breed club and approved by the American Kennel Club until 1958, at which time the standard was once more revised to read:

Size: Desired height 11 inches to 11½ inches at the withers. A dog of either sex measuring under 10 inches and over 12½ inches shall be disqualified.

During the interim, much deliberation and an open exchange of thoughts and ideas took place between breeders in one-on-one debates and through the print media. A great deal of anxiety was expressed that Min Pins were getting too large, that too many different sizes were being shown and winning, and that there was no conformity of size within litters, to name but a few of the areas of concern.

Although the MPCA had voted in 1955 to adopt size disqualifications for the breed, it was not until 1958 that such came to pass. Meanwhile the national breed club was embroiled with internal strife and soon became virtually inactive. It was reorganized in 1964 and has been operating smoothly ever since.

The subject of gait is another item that was not exactly covered in the initial American standard and has undergone much discussion and revamping. The debate continues to this day. The original American standard gave 25 points to General Appearance and Movement, but no direct reference was made to the type of movement desired. Although the initial German standard had said, "quick in movement," this was dropped from the American version. A direct reference to the "hackney" requirement was not made until the full revision of the American standard in 1950. In this version movement increased to 30 points and was given the notation "very important." The introduction said, "The natural characteristic traits which identify him from other toy dogs are his precise Hackney gait, his fearless animation, complete self-possession, and his spirited presence." The words "precise Hackney gait" remained in the breed's American standard until 1980 when it was modified to read, "hackney-like action." This change was made to reflect a more modern thinking that dictates a pushing, driving rear movement with high-stepping, bend at the wrist, forward motion front action. It was felt that the word "precise" meant an animal that lifts its feet high with little push from the rear, hence mincing. Breeders felt that a dog with such action goes nowhere and was wrong for the breed.

Hackney references never existed in any of the German standards and even the current Federation Cynologique Internationale (FCI) standard—which adopts standards from the designated breed country of origin, or in this case Germany—only refers to movement with the requirement that the "Pinscher must trot, not pace, in diagonal sequence." England, however, which is not a full FCI member, elected to adopt the earlier American version and requires "precise hackney gait." It has not amended its standard to reflect the later American compromise of calling for a "hackney-like" action.

The Foundation Dogs and Breeders

As the American standard underwent growth changes, so too did the Miniature Pinscher breed in this country. Many dogs were initially too large, too cumbersome. Then the pendulum swung in the opposite direction, with many appearing as tiny and dwarfish. Each time the standard was altered it was to reflect the need to swing that pendulum back toward the middle. Regardless of these changes, some of the great dogs of the past could step into the ring today and win. Ch. Patzie V. Mill-Mass, owned by Mrs. E.L. Doheny, III, bred by Mrs. Mildred Mastin and shown by Porter Washington of California in the early 1950s, is one example. Patzie amassed a record of 25 Bests in Show, 100 Group 1sts and 140 Bests of Breed in an era when transportation was mostly by car and shows were local.

Other Min Pins that have left their mark either in the show ring or as ancestors in the pedigrees of today's top winners were Int. Ch. King Allah v. Siegenburg, also owned by Mrs. Doheny's Eldomar Kennels; Ch. King Eric von Konigsbach and Ch. Rajah von Siegenburg, both owned by Carolyn Clark Roe; Ch. Jazebel v. Rochburg, owned and bred by the Rochburg Kennels of Dr. and Mrs. Frank W. Hartman and Miss Edna Hartman, Detroit, Michigan, and several Rochburg bitches (Annabelle, Lulubel, Lenlibel, Eribel, Rose, Sophia, Greta and Frieda, to name a few) who were productive in the show ring and whelping box. Two Rochburg homebred studs, Ch. Mitson and Swantz of Rochburg, together with a German import, Ch. Rex von Sterntor, figured highly in the successful Rochburg breeding program.

Jim and Marian Geddes, Geddesburg Kennels, were effective Min Pin breeders who saw the breed through its early growth and

A 1938 champion, Ch. Count Otto v. Montgomery, owned by Dr. Harry A. Shier of Colorado. Courtesy of the American Kennel Club.

Percy Roberts with Ch. Rajah v. Siegenburg, owned by Mrs. William O. Bagshaw. Courtesy of the American Kennel Club.

Ch. King Allah v. Siegenburg is in back of many of today's top-winning Min Pins. It is believed that he sired 84 champions.

Ch. Princess Sylvia v. Konigsbach, one of a long line of famed Konigsbach Min Pins. Courtesy of the American Kennel Club.

Ch. Marlene's Rajah was the son of Ch. Rajah v. Siegenburg. Courtesy of the American Kennel Club.

Ch. Patzie von Mill-Mass was the top-winning Min Pin during the early 1950s.

Ch. Red Duke of Geddesburg was bred by Jim and Marion Geddes. Courtesy of the American Kennel Club.

Porter Washington handles Ch. Patzie von Mill-Mass to Best of Breed in 1954, capturing the famous Sir Ius of the Hill sculpture crafted by Miss Michael Carmichael, center. The judge was Alva Rosenberg.

into stabilization. Ch. Zeta-Finanzhof v. Geddesburg and Ch. King of Hearts of Geddesburg were but two of the many Geddesburg dogs that were successful in the ring and as sires. The Geddes, who were professional handlers as well as Min Pin breeders, did much to promote the breed on the East Coast.

Miss Michael Carmichael's Ch. Sir Ius of the Hill was a beautiful show dog and sire who quickly captured hearts in his native state of Texas. Killed at an early age, Rick, as the dog was called, was immortalized by sculptress Mickey Carmichael in a porcelain statue that was given as a memorial trophy for breed specialties.

Many other dogs and breeders had an impact in the initial years of the breed's acceptance in the United States. The dogs include Ch. Bel-Roc's Dobe von Enztal, Ch. Baron von Anthony von Meyer, Ch. Mudhen's Acre Red Snapper, Ch. Rusty von Enztal, Ch. Sergeant Fritz von Enztal, Ch. Bel-Roc's Snicklefritz von Enztal, Ch. Rebel Roc's Casanova von Kurt, Ch. Bel-Roc's Vanguard, Ch. Jupiter von Kurt, Bel-Roc's Juno von Enztal, Ch. Shieldcrest Cinammon Toast, Ch. Jay-Mac's Moon Eagle, Ch. Rebel Roc's Star Boarder, plus many, many others. The bitches of prominence were Ch. Gypsy of Alema, Rolling Green's Sparkle, Ch. Bo-Mar's Drum Song, Ch. Bo-Mar's Blythe Spirit, Ch. Bel-Roc's Sugar von Enztal, Ch. Reh-Mont's Sweet Georgia Brown, Ch. Rebel Roc's Living Doll, Ch. Jay-Mac's Ramblin' Rose, Ch. Jay-Mac's Silk Stockings, Ch. Jay-Mac's Dream Walking, and the list goes on and on.

Two sets of litters are known to have produced Best in Show winners: Ch. Jay-Mac's Pat Hand and Ch. Jay-Mac's Impossible Dream; Ch. Fillpin's Felicity and Ch. Fillpin's Red Raider. Top producers have been Ch. Bo-Mar's Road Runner with 74 champions, and current star Ch. Carlee Nubby Silk has at least 75 as of this writing with more to come.

Many breeders, who have long since gone, worked hard to

Another dog from Geddesburg breeding. Courtesy of the American Kennel Club.

One Min Pin breeder who is no
longer with us, Lee Abrahams,
left a legacy of striving to breed
beautiful Min Pins.
Ritter

Ch. Jay-Mac's Dream Walking was the 1976 top toy dog in the country. Bred by John McNamara, co-owned by him with Jack and Paulann Phelan and shown by Bob Condon, this beautiful bitch acquired 33 BIS and 129 Group 1sts.

Ch. Carlee Nubby Silk, the current all-time top producer, is owned by Mrs. B. Murray Tucker, Jr. and was bred by Ann Dutton and Carol Garrison.   *Ashbey*

promote and preserve their breed and many present day breeders are striving to carry on the legacies left to them. Several out-of-print books on the breed cover breeders and kennels in detail and individuals interested in this early phase of American Min Pin history should try to secure a copy of *The Complete Miniature Pinscher,* by Viva Leone Ricketts (originally published by Denlinger, its revised edition published by Howell), as well as *Your Miniature Pinscher,* written by Dr. Buris R. Boshell (published by Denlinger). Another good breed book that is hard to find is *The Miniature Pinscher That You May Know,* which was written and privately published by the late Chips Jones, a serious Min Pin breeder. An admirable collection of Miniature Pinscher champions appears in four books written by David Krogh of Portland, Oregon: *King of Toys, 1960–1970, King of Toys, 1970–1980, King of Toys, 1958–1982* and *King of Toys, 1983 Yearbook.* All these books provide excellent breed material for the serious devotee of the Miniature Pinscher.

A 1952 photo of some of the first Min Pins in England. To the left is Lionel Hamilton Renwick with a black and rust bitch; on the right is Hank Heron with a red male owned by Molly Sharpe. The judge is Clair Race.

50

4

Interest in England and Other Countries

ALTHOUGH THE MINIATURE PINSCHER had been established in Germany for hundreds of years and was adopted by the Americans in 1929, it was not until after World War II that England began to take an interest in this spirited little dog. The first known imports were two bitches from the Continent, who were brought through quarantine to England in 1949 by one of the earliest English supporters of the breed, Lionel Hamilton-Renwick, of the renown Birling Kennels. Writing a special article for the English national breed club's 25th anniversary, he recalled his trials and tribulations:

> The first time I ever saw a Miniature Pinscher was in Switzerland in 1937. I suppose I had read about them—but had no idea what they looked like in the flesh. In the garden next to the villa where we lived I was intrigued by several tiny black and tan dogs.
>   I asked the owner what they were and she told me in French-speaking Switzerland they were called Pinscher Nain—though they were of German origin. Looking back I suppose they were pretty poor specimens—rather apple-headed, pop-eyed, very small indeed being only about 8 inches in height. These cheeky, fearless, little dogs fascinated me. Later when I watched these and Dobermans at shows I

Natural eared Ch. Lionlike Red Fire Fox was the top-winning Min Pin in England in 1983. He is owned and bred by Fred and Olive Leonard, England. *Pearce*

Ch. Lionlike Black Sirius is a black and rust English stud owned and bred by Fred and Olive Leonard, England. *Pearce*

made up my mind to import both breeds when we returned to England.

All plans had to be put aside with the outbreak of the war when we returned to England. But with the end of hostilities I decided to start showing again. In 1947 I made a trip to the continent in search of dogs to found my kennel. At this time both breeds were virtually unknown in this country and my quest took me to many European countries. Dogs of any sort were hard to find. Owners of good specimens were unwilling to sell at any price. I began to think I would never find what I wanted. I eventually bought a beautiful, fully police-trained Dobe bitch and three red Miniature Pinscher bitches. I dared not import a black and tan as I felt sure I would be accused of docking English Toy Terriers!

The four bitches were left in Holland to be mated and when in whelp to be flown to this country. The Miniature Pinscher bitches were very unlucky with their puppies. The young uncropped bitch died before whelping and the two older bitches lost all of their puppies, which included four dogs. I was now without a future stud dog. The best bitch, a charming 10½″ red, lost an eye in quarantine, which set up an infection from which she died when released from quarantine. The only thing left to do was to fly back to Holland to look for a dog. This proved a difficult task indeed. Eventually I was fortunate enough to find an outstanding six-month-old dog puppy who was to become my first champion in the breed before flying to England. As he was cropped I knew that he could not be shown here—but he was such a good looker. I decided he should be left in his native country to be shown, even if it meant scrapping breeding plans for a year or so. Campaigning hard on the continent, Birling Tommi v. Charlois was the leading Min Pin in Holland and Belgium. Flown back to England he was eventually mated to my surviving bitch Birling Stockton Kora. Fate was still against me for his first two best puppies died of hardpad at six months old. I repeated this mating and produced Birling Rocket, a lovely prick-eared red dog. I think he appears in nearly every Miniature Pinscher pedigree in this country. Before I could show this dog his two hind legs were terribly scalded by a kettle of boiling water as he lay in front of the fire. He made a wonderful recovery—but showing was out of the question.

One of his daughters, however, made breed history by being the first Min Pin to appear in the Best in Show ring at Crufts. This really put the breed on the map and since then things have gone from strength to strength. So in spite of all the expense and disappointments I think my efforts to help establish the Miniature Pinscher have been a very worthwhile adventure.

Lionel Hamilton-Renwick formally introduced Min Pins to Great Britain and soon other breeders followed in his footsteps, buying dogs not only from the Continent, but America as well. Fred and Julia Curnow, Tavey Kennels, brought the first American-bred Min Pins into England from Jim Geddes of the noted Geddesburg Kennels in New Jersey. One of their in-whelp American imports, Carwyn's Orilla, produced the first British champion. Going to live with Mrs. Molly Sharpe of Scotland, that first champion, Kaama of Tavey, is described by Mrs. Sharpe as "a biggish red, with great style, who moved like a high-stepping horse."

From England, some of the Curnow American-bred Miniature Pinschers were exported to Australia, where they became the first of the breed to be registered in that country. One was a young bitch in whelp to the black-and-tan American dog, Delegate of Geddesburg. This bitch produced the first litter of Australian puppies. As with England, this unique breed caught the fancy of many dog breeders and soon other Min Pins were imported from England, the United States, New Zealand and Germany. One breeder in particular, Mike Towell, Zwergpin Kennels, New South Wales, has experience with both importing from and exporting to Germany. He explains his program:

> The Min Pin reached a peak in popularity and quality in the period of the late 1970s to early 1980s. We had many breeders at that time and many new imports were coming from the United Kingdom. However, due to the predominance of the U.K. influence, we found that fineness of bone was creeping into the breed. Also due to close breeding programs faulty temperament was becoming evident in some lines.
>
> With these two thoughts in mind we opted to import from Germany a brood bitch who was excellent in both temperament and strength of bone. Mated to our dog (an Australian-bred champion) we found that the refinement of the German type was accepted by judges from all over the world and that most major breed awards in recent years have gone to animals from this line when they have been exhibited. Also, with the exportation of this breeding back to Europe

Australian Ch. Zwergpin Sweet 'N Spicy, owned by Mike and Helen Towell of Australia.

Australian Ch. Roepin Bronze Prince, also owned by the Towells.
Dorizas

55

(specifically Germany and England) we found that the line was also well accepted over there with the winning of many major breed and group awards.

From our experience in breeding Min Pins, we found that our German line allowed for very healthy puppies of reasonable size, without the earlier problems of puppy fading. Bitches in the past had a high predominance of aborting litters or tragically puppy fading could and often would set in. Thankfully, we as breeders seem to have all that behind us now.

The development of Min Pins in Israel is based on the blending of lines from more than one country. The principal Min Pin breeders in Israel, the Efrats, Beit Ma'ayan Kennels, describe their efforts:

The Min Pin that was imported from Germany had an excellent head, strong bones, a good bite and an attractive colour but the body was too long for international standards. In 1980, I acquired a male and female from the United States. These dogs had a short body, but their heads, colour and especially their bite caused breeding problems. A second try resulted in the development of good-looking dogs with excellent bodies and good heads. However, with this there were the unexpected problems of poor bites and puppies born with a large range of sizes in each litter.

Today, the Min Pin is the most popular and well-liked dog in Israel. This can be attributed to its size, its short hair and easy temperament. It is suited to houses and to large apartment buildings and is an excellent watch dog and companion.

Breeders in Canada were also quick to adopt the Min Pin. The MacCuaigs, Bates and Sparks are but three active breeders who work hard to preserve and maintain the breed in that country. Gerona MacCuaig, Jethona Kennels, describes the Min Pin as having an "animated appearance that is a pleasure to watch," while Mary Bates, Devileen, says the breed is "very challenging, determined and clever." Many Canadian breeders maintain a close association with their American counterparts and are members of the MPCA. This relationship has been profitable for breeders on both sides of the border. The Canadians have shared in some of America's better breeding programs, and the Americans have

A collection of four Min Pins from Israel that are a combination of German and American bloodlines. Owned and bred by David and Eva Efrat, Israel.

Head study of Dusha Me Beit-Hammayan, owned and bred by David and Eva Efrat, Israel.

Can. & Am. Ch. Devileen's Benzyl Benzoate, Am. CD, Can. CDX, TD, is owned, bred and trained by Mary and Bedford Bates, Canada.

Head study of Can. & Am. Ch. Fillpin's Foxfire, an American dog from the Fillpots' kennels that was sold to Mary and Bedford Bates, Canada.
L. Lindt

58

benefited from having one of Canada's premier Min Pin breeders, Robert Waters, Lo-Bob Kennels, retire to California and pursue an active judging career. Bob Waters, who was an all-breed Canadian judge before moving to the states, is one of the few judges licensed by the American Kennel Club for all breeds in this country.

One of the principal goals that breeders from around the world have had in common was the desire to breed and raise quality dogs within the confines of their respective standards. That the breed is accepted and, indeed, popular, is due to the diligence and support of these individuals.

Bob Waters was a prominent Canadian breeder of Min Pins before his retirement and move to southern California. One of the dogs he bred was Ch. Mystery Gal of Lo-Bob, shown by Anne Rogers Clark. Awarding the dog BOB in 1963 is E.W. Tipton, Jr.

E. Shafer

5

Breeding

IN 1904 RICHARD STREBEL, a leading canine artist, writer and Min Pin breeder from Germany, cautioned in his text, *Die Deutschen Hunde (The German Dog Breeds):*

> The first rule in breeding the Pinscher variety called Miniature Pinscher (Zwergpinscher) should be to breed it in accordance with the same well-proportioned ideal type, the model for which is described in the standard for the Old German Standard Pinscher; it should be an exact miniature replica of the Standard Pinscher.
>
> More and more faults, defects and weaknesses appear in the miniature or toy varieties, the smaller they become. It is, for example, almost impossible to prevent the appearance of dome-shaped skulls and drastically shortened muzzles. . . . One should always breed the bitch to a smaller dog; that way, not so many bitches are lost due to whelping problems. . . . Unfortunately, the abnormal size reduction brings many problems and disadvantages: the tiny ones become more and more delicate and more susceptible to illness and diseases, shiver all day long during the colder months and retract their hindquarters.

What Strebel wrote in 1904 is still true today—you breed dogs with the purpose of developing quality, healthy animals to carry on a given breed. Dr. Buris R. Boshell, of the famed Bo-Mar Kennels in

Alabama, offers this advice to anyone wanting to breed quality Min Pins:

> For successful breeding one must first of all have an eye for a dog, be perfectly honest with themselves and not be kennel blind and, in addition, must have a certain degree of luck.
>
> I hear people talk about genetics and that they follow a very strong genetic line in their breeding program. Actually in view of the fact that it takes several generations to really more or less purify the genes, I have found it important to do phenotypic breeding rather than paper breeding. When we purchased our first bitch, we tested both sides of the pedigree, and we found an ideal breeding was breeding granddaughter to grandfather. After this, we then tended to concentrate on the particular side of the pedigree that gave us the best results. We followed a rather strong line breeding program in this regard. Such a program allowed us to breed 100 or more champions. However, I did find a rather interesting thing in that after I achieved a certain level of success where my dogs strongly resembled each other and we had a kennel full of quality champion bitches, our substance began to disappear as we were breeding like to like, of proper size and substance. Because of this, I found it necessary to go back and breed some opposites and in this regard, we frequently used a large bitch and a small male, but both with good soundness and general overall type and quality. On at least one occasion, however, I used a very small bitch to a medium or slightly large male and achieved considerable success.
>
> Actually, when we pursued this line of breeding one of the first male Miniature Pinschers that really impressed us was Ch. Bel Roc's Dobe Von Enztal. He was a large dog but elegant and racy. He was the sire of Ch. Sargent Fritz Von Enztal, who sired the famous producer, Snicklefritz. Snicklefritz was then the sire of Ch. Bo-Mar's Drummer Boy, and Drummer Boy sired Ch. Bo-Mar's Brandy of Jay-Mac. Brandy then sired the top producer of all times, Ch. Bo-Mar's Road Runner. I believe that Road Runner has sired more than 80 champions, a mark that will probably stand for a long period of time.

Another prominent breeder was John McNamara, of the renown Jay-Mac Kennels in Illinois. McNamara, who no longer breeds or shows Min Pins, looks back on the time he and his wife devoted to breeding quality dogs as being proud, productive years.

Dr. Buris Boshell, with Ch. Rebel Roc's Star Boarder, believes a successful breeder must have an eye for a dog, be honest and not kennel blind, and have a certain degree of luck. *Ritter*

Ch. Bo-Mar's Drummer Boy, co-owned by Buris Boshell and John McNamara, was a top winner and important stud dog. He was shown by Clara Alford. *Alexander*

Several current breeders give the McNamaras credit for establishing a line of Min Pins that drastically altered the breed in America during the 1960s. At 81 years of age, John McNamara is still fresh of spirit and mind. He offers the following poignant advice based on his own experiences:

The Miniature Pinscher is a rather hard breed to breed to the standard and to the standard we set for ourselves. We decided early that we would breed the type we wanted and liked, no matter what the odds were. Since I came from a family that has bred fine saddle horses for over 100 years, I thought that a fine Miniature Pinscher should have the same clean lines and silhouette as a fine saddle mare. The long arched neck and the thin chiselled head with alert ears, the good top line, high tailset and, above all, four good legs set in the correct position. This is the standard for the American-bred saddle horse and that was the type of Min Pin I wanted. With this picture in my mind, I would not rest until I had attained at least part of my vision or goal.

Forty or so years ago, many of the Min Pins were short, cobby little dogs with heavy heads and necks and rather short legs. In many cases, they lacked the elegance or style that we wanted. There are some breeders who liked and bred that type of Min Pin, claiming that was the true German Miniature Pinscher, but we did not care for that type.

After a couple of false starts with pet-types and a good male from Tipton that we finished quite quickly, we sold all the stock we had and brought two of the best Miniature Pinscher bitches we could find from Dr. Boshell. They were definitely show-puppies and the very tops in breeding. One bitch was a double Von Kurt breeding and the other one a Von Kurt and Alema cross. Both bitches finished their championships quickly and were ready to be bred on their second season. In looking for suitable studs to mate them with, we decided to go to Tipton's Ch. Rebel Roc's Casanova v Kurt with one of them and the Booher's Ch. Bel Roc's Dobe with the other bitch, as they were the two top studs in the country, with real quality breeding in depth. In those breedings we also picked up many of the famous old lines that had done so much for the breed. From those two matings we got some real nice puppies and felt we were on the way. We never bred both bitches to the same stud and thus developed two lines that we could criss-cross breed in developing our own line. I had learned from my father's horse breeding never to skimp on the stud; even if you have to hock your coat, go to the best.

Ch. Jay-Mac's Ramblin' Rose, owned and bred by Mr. and Mrs. John R. McNamara, was one of the breed's top-producing bitches and behind a lot of today's winners. *Booth*

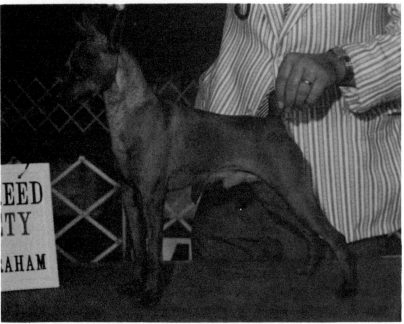

One of Ramblin' Rose's successful offspring was multi-BIS winner Ch. Jay-Mac's Pat Hand. *Graham*

The way was not all success, as we found some judges did not like our racy type of Min Pin with the longer ears and longer tail, along with the longer neck and longer legs. However, some did like them and we continued to try to improve on that type. We tried above all not to be kennel blind and to cull, if they did not come up to or produce what we had in mind. If they did not meet the requirements, they were moved out.

We kept for our breeding stock only our top show bitches and if we can point to any one reason why we have had some success, good bitches would be our answer. If we found a better stud dog outside our kennel, we went to him without regard to expense or convenience. Each generation must be an improvement or bring us some of the qualities that we had as our goal, as we constantly tried to move forward.

We found one major problem in breeding good Min Pins and that was in controlling the size. In a litter of three, there would often be one big one, a middle-sized and a small one. We improved somewhat on that problem, but could not completely eliminate it. We felt the problem came from some breeders who tried to keep real large bitches for good easy whelpers and large litters when bred to small studs. We tried to stay with the average 11½" size in both studs and bitches. We would not breed to any stud, no matter how good he may have been as an individual, unless his pedigree went back and tied into some of the fine old lines that did the winning fifty years ago. We found that shallow breeding did not produce quality.

We believed that the Miniature Pinscher had to be very outstanding to go out and compete in the Toy Groups as long-coats gave us real competition. He had to be alert with head and tail held high and move with assurance that he's "it" and in the right places. The Min Pin has no long coat to catch the judge's eye or cover possible faults. The Min is out there in his underwear, he's all hung out for the world to see. If a foot turns in or out, it's obvious to the judge as well as the ringside. If a leg arcs rather than drives, it's soon caught. In other words, the show Min Pin has to have the soundness and elegance bred into him, to be able to compete.

McNamara's philosophy regarding the breeding of Miniature Pinschers was certainly successful for him. His homebred Ch. Jay-Mac's Impossible Dream, owned by Dorothy De Maria and shown by Joe Waterman, still, with more than ten years passing since retirement, holds the breed record for winning bitches with 79 Bests

65

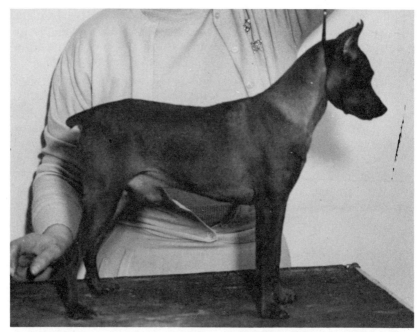

Ch. Baron Anthony von Meyer was described by E.W. Tipton as "the ugliest little Min Pin I ever saw," yet he produced over 20 champions out of Rolling Greens Sparkle, including "Little Daddy."

Ch. Rebel Roc's Vanguard von Kurt, left, and Ch. Rebel Roc's Geronimo, right, were other "Tony" and "Sparkle" sons.

Linda Kazan Stevens bred and showed top winner Ch. King Pin's Hawkeye.

A Sparkle son by Ch. Tip Topper was Ch. Rebel Roc's Billy von Kurt.   *Shafer*

67

Ch. Von Dort's Dominator, top, and Ch. Von Dorf's Stylish Stepper, bottom, are products of the Grusendorf's careful breeding program, which combined the Rebel Roc, Bel-Roc and Bo-Mar lines.

in Show to her credit. (E.W. Tipton's dog, Ch. Rebel Roc's Cassanova Von Kurt, holds the male record with 75 Bests in Show.) Other McNamara bitches, such as Ch. Jay-Mac's Ramblin' Rose and her daughter, Ch. Jay-Mac's Silk Stockings, have been out of top producers and have become top producers themselves. Many of the winning dogs today can trace their lines back to Jay-Mac dogs.

McNamara is concerned about a present day practice of some breeders to ignore the quality of the bitch and just seek out a top-winning stud:

> Lately, I've seen many show entries out of no-name, no-champion, no-breeding bitches but a top stud. They apparently think the good stud can pick up the quality. It can't be done that way.
> Mortgage your soul if necessary to start with a great mother that will give you a dozen ways to succeed.

Linebreeding is another aspect to consider when trying to produce quality Min Pins. Kent and Nancy Grusendorf, of Von Dorf Kennels in Texas, are strong advocates of a closely watched linebreeding program coupled with a valuable stud dog. They attribute their success with a small kennel to a handful of major, equally important ingredients:

> Select each stud dog based on his show record, his ability to perpetuate assets and overcome faults, maintaining a linebred family (within three generations) always with the largest percentage of that linebreeding coming from multi-best in show winners and always breeding to maintain type and for improvement.

The Grusendorfs offer this formula for determining line-breeding coefficiency:

> 1. Within the first 4 generations, list the common ancestors.
> 2. Then add the generations in which the common ancestor appears. If a common ancestor appears in the 1st, 3rd and 4th generation, calculate as follows:

$$1 + 3 = 4$$

$$1 + 4 = 5$$

3. Then subtract 1 from each, i.e.:

$$1 + 3 = 4 - 1 = 3$$

$$1 + 4 = 5 - 1 = 4$$

4. Equate the resulting figures into a percentile value based upon the following schedule:

2 = 25.00%	4 = 6.25%	6 = 1.57%
3 = 12.50%	5 = 3.13%	7 = .75%

Example: $1 + 3 = 4 - 1 = 3 = 12.50\%$

$1 + 4 = 5 - 1 = 4 = 6.25\%$

5. Add together the percentile figures for all common ancestors as indicated above to obtain total *linebreeding coefficiency:* .75% to 25.00% is linebreeding, 26.00% and up is inbreeding.

We try to maintain as close to 25% as possible with the largest part of the 25% coming from a multi-best in show dog, and always breeding to maintain type and for improvement. This formula was the foundation for every litter we planned as shown in the example in Figure 5.1.

Selecting the proper stud dog to mate to a quality bitch is important. Two other breeders who adhere to this philosophy are Irvine "Buddy" and Linda Kazan Stevens, long-time successful Kentucky Min Pin breeders, using before their marriage the banner of Bud-Lee Kennels for Buddy and King Pin for Linda. They combined their talents and established Redwing Kennels in 1987:

We personally prefer fairly tight linebreeding. It is our opinion that to breed two animals who are completely unrelated is to ask for trouble.

If at all possible, we want to see the prospective sire in person. Pictures are not always a great help in evaluating an animal. Much can also be learned if the prospective sire's parents are available to be observed.

It is necessary to make a mental or written list of the features most liked in the bitch and the prospective sire. It is necessary that one be strong where the other is weak. Never breed two animals with a common fault. Just as we lock in the finer points, so too can we lock in the faults of the animals mated.

70

Figure 5.1. Four Generation Pedigree

```
                        Bel-Roc's Snicklefritz v. Enztal
              Ch. Bo-Mar's Drummer Boy
                      ꞏ Ch. Bo-Mar's Ebony Belle
      Ch. Bo-Mar's Brandy of Jay-Mac
                        Ch. Rebel Roc's Jupiter v. Kurt
              Ch. Bo-Mar's Blythe Spirit
                        Ch. Rebel Roc's Cora v. Kurt
CH. BO-MAR'S ROAD RUNNER
                        Ch. Baron Anthony v. Meyer
              Ch. Rebel Roc's Casanova v. Kurt
                        Rolling Green's Sparkle
      Bo-Mar's Dancing Doll
                        Ch. Rebel Roc's Jupiter v. Kurt
              Ch. Bo-Mar's Drum Song
                        Ch. Bo-Mar's Ebony Belle


                        Ch. Jay-Mac's Blue Chips
              Ch. Jay-Mac's Band Wagon
                        Ch. Jay-Mac's High Society
      Ch. Jay-Mac's Candy Man
                        Ch. Bo-Mar's Drum Song of Jay-Mac
              Ch. Jay-Mac's Ramblin Rose
                        Ch. Bo-Mar's Drum Song
CH. VON DORF'S STYLISH STEPPER
                        Ch. Bo-Mar's Brandy of Jay-Mac
              Ch. Bo-Mar's Road Runner
                        Bo-Mar's Dancing Doll
      Ch. Jay-Mac's Caroline
                        Ch. Rebel Roc's Jackpot
              Am. & Can. Ch. Jay-Mac's Jacqueline
                        Jay-Mac's Jasmin
```

List of common ancestors:

1. Ch. Bo-Mar's Road Runner	:	1 + 3 = 4 − 1 = 3 = 12.50%
2. Ch. Bo-Mar's Brandy of Jay-Mac	:	2 + 4 = 6 − 1 = 5 = 3.13%
3. Bo-Mar's Dancing Doll	:	2 + 4 = 6 − 1 = 5 = 3.13%
4. Ch. Bo-Mar's Drum Song	:	3 + 4 = 7 − 1 = 6 = 1.57%
5. Ch. Bo-Mar's Ebony Belle	:	4 + 4 = 8 − 1 = 7 = .75%
6. Ch. Rebel Roc's Juniper v. Kurt	:	4 + 4 = 8 − 1 = 7 = .75%
LINEBREEDING COEFFICIENCY TOTAL	:	21.83%

71

Ideally we like to breed animals who are close in the first three generations. However, sometimes we must go outside one of the lines to bring in features which we feel are vital to the improvement of a given line.

The stud dog must complement the bitch in as many areas as possible. It is our belief that the bitch is the more important of the two. Too much credit is given to the sire in many instances. We feel that the bitch is 70–75% responsible for the quality of most litters.

Some sires, due to their show records or popularity, create very impressive lists of champion offspring. However, the true worth is determined not solely in champions but rather in the ratio of champion puppies versus pet puppies.

Breeding of animals is a great responsibility and should not be taken lightly. We find more and more persons breeding any dog to any bitch and this can destroy the breed. For the most part, 15 years ago when you attended a show with 45 Min Pins entered, not over three or four sires were represented. Today, with a like entry, there can be 30 to 35 different males used.

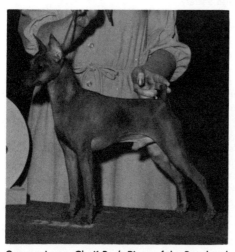

Group winner, Ch. K-Roc's Piece of the Roc, bred and owned by David and Sharon Krogh, Oregon.
Lindemaier

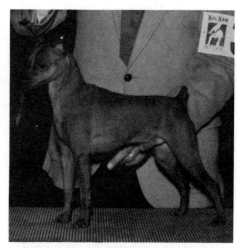

Multi-BIS winner, Ch. Ruffian Starback, bred and owned by Larry and Penny Dewey, Texas.
Petrulis

6

A Conversation Between
Two Old-timers

MANY SUCCESSFUL BREEDERS are more than willing to help and advise other breeders who are earnestly striving to improve their breed. One of the best ways to learn and understand a particular breed is to talk with some of the prominent breeders who have many years of experience with the breed. Given the vastness of the country, this is not always feasible.

In the fall of 1986 renown breeder E.W. Tipton, Jr., of Rebel Roc Kennels, an American Kennel Club licensed all-breed judge, sat down with his old friend Maisie Booher (now Summers) of Bel-Roc Kennels in West Virginia and talked about Min Pins. These two old-timers exchanged personal thoughts, ideas and criticisms in a typical conversation that could take place between two knowledgeable breeders of any breed, any place in the world. Tipton tape-recorded the conversation for this book so that all who are interested in Min Pins would be able to learn from their forthright exchange of personal experiences, concepts and impressions. Within seven months, E.W. Tipton, Jr. had passed away but he left behind this conversational legacy for the Min Pin world:

BOOHER: My first Min Pin was just a pet. Then I got a second one from Hank Reed, who was a professional handler, and then also through him my first bitch for breeding. I got Rusty [Ch. Rusty von Enztal] in 1950 when he was already six years old. Dobe [Ch. Bel-Roc's Dobe von Enztal] was born in 1951.

TIPTON: To me, Dobe was the turning point of bringing elegance into Min Pins.

BOOHER: I think that's because so many of the Min Pins before then were apple headed, short of neck and very low on leg without much elegance. They were mostly solid, cobby little dogs.

TIPTON: Who was Dobe's sire and dam?

BOOHER: Ch. Rusty von Enztal and Reedlynde Red Flame.

TIPTON: And Dobe sired Sugar [Ch. Bel-Roc's Sugar von Enztal]?

BOOHER: That's right.

TIPTON: That's when we began to get the longer necks, different type head and proper gait and proper tail set, and so forth.

BOOHER: And Sugar's dam was like a bitch I got from Adam Strauss, who used to be president of the Min Pin Club. Some of his dogs were a little bit larger, but they did have neck, head and a lot of the substance we like in a Min Pin, except they were too large and we had to reduce the size.

TIPTON: Was there disqualification in those days on size?

BOOHER: No, not then.

TIPTON: When did the disqualification come into being as nearly as you remember?

BOOHER: I would say, maybe 1958. They changed the standard to include under 10 inches and over 12½. Dobe was just a fraction over 12½ inches but he was already finished by then. I always felt, and still do, that the better dog came from the top half of the standard, 11 inches and up and the 10-inch dogs went back to the Chihuahua type.

TIPTON: Right, I agree with you 100%. Do you think the Min Pins we are seeing at shows today are better than the ones of 15 or 20 years ago? Do you think the Min Pin breed has improved over the past 15 years?

BOOHER: No, I don't. I think that they're losing some of the hackney gait. They have bred for too much refinement and they're losing depth of chest and rib spring and they're a little longer backed than we liked to have. Weakness in the rear is also a problem today.

TIPTON: Do you think the head is as good as it used to be?

BOOHER: I haven't seen too many heads that went back to the really old type of head, but the heads are getting a little bit snipier.

TIPTON: I think some are trying to breed a Doberman type head and this is wrong as far as I am concerned.

BOOHER: The nose is too long and too much drop under the eyes.

TIPTON: That's right. There is not enough fill under the eyes.

BOOHER: Right.

TIPTON: What do you think needs to be done to bring the breed back to the prominence that it was?

BOOHER: Well, I think breeders who have long backed, shallow dogs, even though they may have some of the qualities we like, should try not breeding those dogs to each other because like begets like. They should try striving to breed for a smaller dog, more filled out in the rib cage, more shortness of back and less space in the loin. I think that we've got to have a balance. I don't think we can keep breeding these leggy dogs to leggy dogs to leggy dogs forever and expect to keep the type.

TIPTON: I agree with you. Maisie, of the dogs that you have seen over the past many years, tell me something about the ones that you consider to be the better dogs that did more for the breed than the others. And I'm going to ask you to include your own dogs because you certainly had a great deal to do with the improvement of the breed as far as the refinement and style and so forth with Dobe, Fritz [Ch. Sergeant Fritz v. Enztal] and the others.

BOOHER: I think that one of the most contributing dogs to the breed as it was maybe ten or more years ago was Dobe, because he did bring the elegance of head and neck to a lot of his offspring, and he was prolific in passing that on to the second and third generation. His get and theirs still have that good

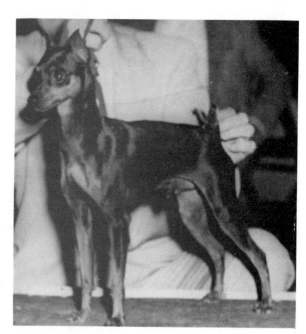

One of the breed's great early producers was Ch. Bel-Roc's Dobe v. Enztal.

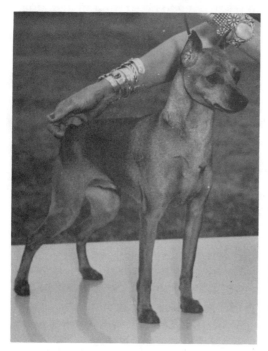

His daughter, Ch. Bel-Roc's Sugar von Enztal, bred by the Boohers and owned by the Tiptons, figured prominently in the Tipton's Rebel Roc breeding program.
Shafer

One of Sugar's daughters was Ch. Rebel Roc's Living Doll, a multi-BIS winner shown taking the Toy Group at International Kennel Club in Chicago. Handler was Anne Rogers (Clark) and the judge was Heywood Hartley.   *Ritter*

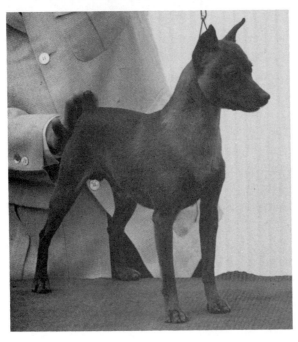

Ch. Mudhen Acres Red Snapper was a BIS winner who was a top sire for Ann Dutton, Sanbrook Kennels.

Frasie Studio

head and neck. Then, of course, I have to go back to the original old Rusty [Ch. Rusty v. Enztal] because it was his pedigree that did the most for my breeding program, and I think he had some of the really great dogs behind him like King Eric [Ch. King Eric von Koningsbach] and Prince [Ch. Rajah von Siegenburg]. Those dogs were of the type I like. I know that Rusty, though he was born in 1945, was more the type Min Pin I like, even today, than so many of the other old time dogs were. Perhaps he didn't do as well then because he was different.

TIPTON: He was ahead of his time, would you say?

BOOHER: That's right. Different than those little apple-headed Min Pins being shown at that time. Pearl Baum had some good dogs, like Little Tulip [Ch. Baum's Little Tulip]. She had some good black and tans. I never did like the dog she had brought from Germany. In my opinion, he was the type we were trying to get away from and so we were going back to the old time dogs. Then with the cross between Tony [Ch. Baron Anthony von Meyer] and Sparkle [Rolling Greens Sparkle] out came Little Daddy [Ch. Rebel Roc's Casanova von Kurt] and Vanguard [Ch. Rebel Roc's Vanguard von Kurt] and the good dogs produced by those two did a lot for the breed. My Dobe produced Fritz, Fritz sired Snicklefritz [Bel-Roc's Snicklefritz v. Enztal], and he sired Drummer Boy [Ch. Bo-Mar's Drummer Boy] and Drum Call [Ch. Bo-Mar's Drum Call]. I thought Drum Call was better than Drummer Boy.

TIPTON: I did too. You remember I put Drum Call up at the specialty over Drummer Boy.

BOOHER: Ann Dutton has had some good dogs, very good dogs. I don't remember all the names now, but I think Ann is one who has kept the substance and still bred for an elegant dog—sound, good Min Pins. I think she is really one of the concerned people who kept in the breed and is trying to keep the breed as it should be.

TIPTON: How did you rank Impossible Dream [Ch. Jay-Mac's Impossible Dream], the one that Joe Waterman showed in California? Where does she come in?

BOOHER: Let's see, Impossible Dream did well as a show dog. I think she was a beautiful bitch, not the quality of Casanova [Ch. Rebel Roc's Casanova von Kurt] and not the quality of some of the others who didn't do as much winning as she did, but she had showmanship. She knew how to present herself. To me, she was a little long in back and a little lacking in tail set and overall didn't have quite the soundness of some of the other dogs. Yet, you couldn't help but love her because she was so good for the breed as far as promoting the breed was concerned. I'm trying to think of other good dogs, but I've been away too long. There were so many good dogs I've forgotten, and can't mention them all.

TIPTON: You had a black and tan that I thought was one of the prettiest dogs I've ever seen—Snicklefritz. He did a great deal as a sire for the breed over the years.

BOOHER: I think he sired about 23 champions in all. He and Dobe were about even in siring champion Min Pins.

TIPTON: Hank Hearn's dog, Red Snapper [Ch. Mudhen Acres Red Snapper], did a great deal for the breed.

BOOHER: He sure did and he did a lot for Sanbrook. He was there at the start of her kennel.

TIPTON: And gave them their start in really good breeding type.

BOOHER: That's right. He was good. And Cinnamon Toast [Ch. Bailes Cinnamon Toast] was a good little dog and did a lot of winning. Cinny, I think, sired over 20 champions. I don't know exactly the number he sired, but he gave a lot to the breed. He wasn't exactly the type that I was really crazy about, but he was above average. He didn't rank in the same class as Casanova or some of the other dogs that have done well for Min Pins, but he was a nice dog. Roadie [Ch. Bo-Mar's Road Runner] was a good dog.

TIPTON: Yes, he was. I thought he was an elegant dog, a beautiful dog.

BOOHER: Beautiful and he did a lot for the breed.

TIPTON: Yes, as a sire and a show dog, too. I think Mr. and Mrs. Kleinmanns did a big service to the breed in showing that dog as

79

Maisie Booher (Summers) is handling her homebred Ch. Bel-Roc's Buster Brown to a Min Pin national specialty BOB at Trenton Kennel Club in 1962. The judge was E.W. Tipton, Jr., and the trophy was presented by William Kleinmanns. Carl French is standing to the left of Maisie Booher Summers.   *Gilbert*

Ch. Rusty v. Enztal, owned by Maisie Booher.

they did. In your opinion, what has happened over the years to set the Min Pins back? I mean tell me about heads, tell me about gait, about body and so forth.

BOOHER: Well, one thing I think breeders were trying to do was breed dogs that looked too much like Dobermans. They were too high on their legs. They had too much neck and naturally too much neck is going to have too long of a head. In breeding for that, they lost depth of chest and so many dogs were so narrow in the front they looked as though both front legs came out of the same socket. With the long back, they were over-angulated in the rear and when they gaited their hind legs crossed. This throws them off balance. From the side view and standing at the end of the lead, they looked nice. But watching them coming and going, shows the defect in the gait.

One of my biggest gripes has been ear trim. I think when the breeders started trimming Min Pin's ears clear out to the end of the ear and the dog comes out with his ears flying in the breeze, it spoils the look of his head entirely.

TIPTON: I have been of the opinion for the past many years that the Min Pin's ear is too long and, in some cases, as much as a half an inch too long. It spoils the whole outlook and expression of the dog.

BOOHER: When you see a dog gaiting toward you with his ears flapping like a Papillon, it doesn't look like a Min Pin. I also think they've done a lot to take away from the expression of the head by the ear trim. Of course, it is a man-made thing and can be corrected. As far as the bodies are concerned, if breeders do not stop breeding dogs with such little substance the breed is going to deteriorate.

TIPTON: I've heard it said that the current crop of breeders is trying to change the whole appearance of Min Pins and they don't want them to look anything like they did 15 or 20 years ago. They want a longer, racier type dog. Do you know anything about that?

BOOHER: I haven't heard anything about that. I know that for years they have tried to get the hackney-like gait taken out of the standard. Of course, I think when the standard just said hackney gait it was deceiving, but hackney-like gait is a proper description because that is one of the breed's strong points and one of the things everyone should look for. When they try to take that away, they're going to make the front too straight and are going to have a more terrier type gait than they have now.

TIPTON: You see very few Min Pins today who lift their foot up when they move, or if they do then they don't reach forward. At the same token, in my opinion, they don't drive enough behind to push a topline up like it should be.

BOOHER: I agree with that perfectly. And I'll tell you another thing I think about people in clubs who try to change standards. Whenever you see a lot of breeders trying for a standard change, it's because they are not trying to raise dogs to comply with the standard that's already set by the AKC. They want the standard changed to fit the dog they are raising.

TIPTON: You're exactly right. That's why I've always said that I wish the AKC would not even allow a breed club to write a standard. I think there ought to be a standards committee that would be impartial and write the standard in a short, concise way and get rid of all these ambiguous terms.

BOOHER: There are things in the Min Pin standard, and in every standard that you read, that are double-talk and unnecessary. But, basically, the standard as it is now is all right. If it were just shortened a little bit and made more understandable. There is nothing wrong with the present Min Pin standard, except for size. I wish they would eliminate the 10 inches and go from 10½ to 12½ inches because that is a two-inch leeway in a toy dog and you only have a two-inch leeway in the Doberman standard. You put a 10-inch Min Pin in the ring and a 12½-inch Min Pin in the ring and they look like Mutt and Jeff.

TIPTON: Thank you, Maisie.

At the end of this taped conversation with Maisie Booher (now Summers), Tipton added a few words of his own regarding his concern for the present day Min Pins:

82

I think they are shallow. I think there is no drive, no reach. I don't think they've got any depth of chest and the head certainly leaves something to be desired. I think you could put their heads through a key hole. Some of the breeders today say that the type dog they are breeding is the progressive type Min Pin. Somebody recently told me that and I couldn't help but say, "It's a damn funny thing to me that I could take the wrong type of Min Pin and set a record that will never be broken by any Min Pin, when they can't take their progressive type Min Pins and do any winning to speak of at all.

Tipton later said the discussion regarding progressive type took place in Canada and when he returned to Canada to judge a few months later the breeder told him that he had thought about their conversation and said that Tip had been right—progressive was not better.

The classic Miniature Pinscher—Ch. Casanova von Kurt, owned by E.W. Tipton, Jr.

Brown

The so-called "Continental type." *Shafer*

7

A View of the Standard

SUCCESSFUL BREEDERS KNOW that serious thought and consideration must surround the mating of any quality animals. It is not only necessary to talk with other breeders seeking advice and potentially compatible mates, it is also vital to have a clear, concise understanding of the breed's standard. The following is the current American standard for the Miniature Pinscher, as approved July 8, 1980.

General Appearance—The Miniature Pinscher is structurally a well-balanced, sturdy, compact, short-coupled, smooth-coated dog. He naturally is well groomed, proud, vigorous and alert. Characteristic traits are his hackney-like action, fearless animation, complete self-possession, and his spirited presence.

Head—In correct proportion to the body. Tapering, narrow with well-fitted but not too prominent foreface which balances with the skull. No indication of coarseness. *Skull*—Appears flat, tapering forward toward the muzzle. *Muzzle*—Strong rather than fine and delicate, and in proportion to the head as a whole. Head well-balanced with only a slight drop to the muzzle, which is parallel to the top of the skull. *Nose*—Black only, with the exception of chocolates, which should have a self-colored nose. *Teeth*—Meet in a

Head study of a German
dog.

A Collection of American Head Studies

Ch. Jay-Mac's Dream Walking, owned and bred
by John McNamara, co-owned with Jack and
Paulann Phalen.   *Booth*

Ch. Patzie von Mill-Mass.   *Roberts*

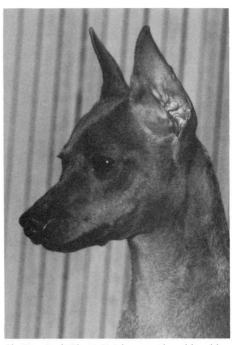

Ch. Larcon's Lit'l Wrecking Crew, owned by Amy Putnam and Connie Wick.   *Candids by Connie*

Ch. Bee Jay's Photo Finish, owned and bred by Bob and Billie Jean Shuler.

Ch. Rebel Roc's Star Boarder, owned by Dr. Buris Boshell, bred by E.W. Tipton.   *Ritter*

Bud-Lee's Spittin Image, owned and bred by Buddy Stevens.

scissors bite. *Eyes*—Full, slightly oval, clear, bright and dark even to the true black, including eye rims, with the exception of chocolates, whose eye rim should be self-colored. *Ears*—Set high, standing erect from base to tip. May be cropped or uncropped. *Lips and Cheeks*—Small, taut and closely adherent to each other.

Neck and Body—*Neck*—Proportioned to head and body, slightly arched, gracefully curved, blending into shoulders, muscular and free from suggestion to dewlap or throatiness. *Topline*—Back level or slightly sloping toward the rear both when standing and gaiting. Length of males equals height at withers. Females may be slightly longer. *Chest and Ribs*—Body compact, slightly wedge-shaped, muscular with well-sprung ribs. Depth of brisket, the base line of which is level with points of elbows. *Loin*—Short and strong in loin with belly moderately tucked up to denote grace of structural form. *Croup*—Level with topline. *Tail*—Set high, held erect, docked in proportion to size of dog.

Forequarters—*Forechest*—Well-developed. *Shoulders*—Clean and sloping with moderate angulation coordinated to permit the hackney-like action. *Legs*—Strong bone development and small clean joints. As viewed from the front, straight and upstanding, elbows close to the body. *Pasterns*—Strong, perpendicular. *Feet*—Small, cat-like, toes strong, well arched and closely knit with deep pads. *Nails*—Thick, blunt. *Dewclaws*—Should be removed from both front and hind legs.

Hindquarters—Well-muscled quarters set wide enough apart to fit into a properly balanced body. As viewed from the rear, the legs are straight and parallel. From the side, well-angulated. *Thighs*—Well-muscled. *Stifles*—Well defined. *Hocks*—Short, set well apart.

Coat—Smooth, hard and short, straight and lustrous, closely adhering to and uniformly covering the body.

Color—Solid clear red. Stag red (red with intermingling of black hairs). Black with sharply defined rust-red markings on cheeks lips, lower jaw, throat, twin spots above eyes and chest, lower half of forelegs, in side of hind legs and vent region, lower portion of hocks and feet. Black pencil stripes on toes. Chocolate with rust-red markings the same as specified for black's except brown pencil stripes on toes. In the solid red and stag red a rich vibrant medium to dark shade is preferred.

Disqualifications: Any color other than listed. Thumb mark (patch of black hair surrounded by rust on the front of the foreleg between the foot and the wrist; on chocolates, the patch is chocolate hair). White on any part of dog which exceeds one-half (½) inch in its longest dimension.

Gait—The forelegs and hind legs move parallel, with feet turning neither in nor out. The hackney-like action is a high-stepping, reaching, free and easy gait in which the front leg moves straight forward and in front of the body and the foot bends at the wrist. The dog drives smoothly and strongly from the rear. The head and tail are carried high.

Size—Ten (10) inches to twelve and one-half (12½) inches in height allowed, with desired height eleven (11) inches to eleven and one-half (11½) inches as measured at highest point of shoulder blades.

Disqualification: Under ten (10) inches or over twelve and one-half (12½) inches in height.

DISQUALIFICATIONS

Any color other than listed. Thumb mark (patch of black hair surrounded by rust on the front of the foreleg between the foot and the wrist; on chocolates, the patch is chocolate hair). White on any part of dog which exceeds one-half (½) inch in its longest dimension.

Under ten (10) inches or over twelve and one-half (12½) inches in height.

The Min Pin standard attempts to define with words, as clearly as possible, the structure of the breed. It is up to the breeders to try to breed dogs to fit that standard. However, as with most standards there are allowances for different interpretations of breed type. With Min Pins that difference primarily centers on body substance. Some American breeders believe the breed should be sturdy and chunky, similar to the type prevalent in continental European dogs, while

A hackney pony lifts its front feet very high and has no rear drive. This pony is owned by Mr. and Mrs. Kenneth Harris.
J. Mellin

A 3½-month-old Min Pin puppy demonstrates that the hackney-like action with the bend at the wrist and good rear drive is an inherent gait.
Candids by Connie

BIS and national specialty winner Ch. Pevenseys Cash Dividend, owned by Pam Ruggie and Marcia Tucker, demonstrates his hackney-like action.
Dave Ashbey

90

Ch. Carovel's Morning Glory, owned and bred by Caroline Ofenloch, shows a high-stepping, driving gait.   *Ashbey*

Ch. King Pins Gate 'n Dancer, owned by Larry and Penny Dewey and bred by Linda Stevens, steps out.

others desire a sleekness of body, which is sometimes defined as racy. The sleek, racy, elegant Min Pin is the type usually seen in the United States and is generally more accepted than the other.

One Canadian breeder, Jean M. Sparks, alludes to the confusion sometimes caused by the two different Min Pin types that exist in North America: "If you have the two different types in the ring, they almost look like two different breeds." Breeders everywhere need to be careful that they do not overly emphasize either an extra lean dog or a heavy, chunky one. A spindly Min Pin is just as wrong as a coarse animal. Breed style, elegance, substance and soundness should never be lost to one particular entity.

Definition of head style is also a problem, as the standard does not refer to the "fill" around the eyes that many older breeders believe is necessary for a proper head. Old-timers always used the standard as a guide for perfection and frequently passed from one to another some of the unwritten breed aspects. The desire to have a degree of chiseling around the eyes is just one example of something that was vital to a good Min Pin head yet never specifically mentioned in the breed standard.

The most controversial section of the Min Pin standard centers on the phrase "hackney-like action." There seems to be two main schools of thought on this subject. Is the "hackney" the true high step with a bend at the wrist similar to that seen in a hackney pony or does hackney refer to high-stepping action without the necessity for any wrist bend? Breeders who have lines that produce the wrist bend, or were attracted to the breed specifically because of this movement, say the former, while those whose dogs step high in front without any bending at the wrist say the latter.

It was not until 1950 that the word "hackney" was added to the American standard. No one seems to know why the gait was not clearly defined in earlier versions. Speculation surrounding the 1950 inclusion centers on the fact that the entire standard has been rewritten at that time and breeders felt it necessary to define with words the required front action, which had become a trademark of the breed in America. With this thought in mind, breeders of the day added to the standard the words "precise hackney gait." A literal

92

interpretation of the word *hackney* without qualifiers, however, proved to be troublesome. A precise hackney gait, as seen in a hackney pony, is a movement that hardly goes anywhere—a lot of action within a little space and no drive. This was not the true gait desired by Min Pin breeders. In 1980, there was finally a consensus of opinion to slightly alter the standard to state "hackney-like action." This phrase was meant to describe a gait that required the dog to naturally lift his front feet up and out with a bend at the wrist while pushing or driving from the behind. The dog should be able to move quickly and smoothly forward with a minimum of effort. This was not to be interpreted as a mincing gait, or as a desire to promote dogs whose front assemblies were out at the elbows and loose in shoulders. In order for the hackney-like gait to properly step out the topline must remain level and the rear legs should propel the animal forward. Sloping toplines and weak, crossing rears indicate a lack of proper bone structure and inability to drive from the rear.

Some present day breeders believe the "hackney-like" phrase is improper for the dogs who cannot bend at the wrist on the forelegs. Indeed, the term most prevalently used by Min Pin breeders to describe a driving gait with high-lifting straight forearms that thrust outward and angulated stifles that push from the rear is "goosestep." A lot of Min Pins cover the ground quickly, highly goosestepping without weaving or crossing and some breeders maintain that this is the correct action. It is the terminology in the standard that they think is misleading.

Some breeders who do not care for the "hackney-like" requirement also state that this is an artificial gait. They maintain that the hackney pony is taught to move that way through the use of weighted shoes. Kenneth Harris, a breeder of show hackney ponies, says this is not necessarily true. Quality hackney ponies are born to move with a hackney action. While weighted shoes might be used to exaggerate a natural action that the pony already possesses, one without such action cannot be contrived to hackney in front regardless of artificial means. He attributes good hackney action to bloodlines and a pony with the proper inherited gait needs little training.

93

The standard provides for specific breed disqualifications. These disqualifications are in addition to the general disqualifications directed by the American Kennel Club. General disqualifications apply to all breeds and prohibit show eligibility for dogs that are blind, deaf, surgically altered, vicious, and for males lacking two testicles in the scrotum.

Specific Min Pin disqualifications cover aspects that the parent breed club considers a definite "no no." There are reasons for each of the designated taboos. As already discussed, the size factor plays an important part in keeping the Miniature Pinscher a small toy dog without dwarfish tendencies. The disqualifying thumb mark, or thumbprint, which is a concentration of black hairs (or chocolate in the case of chocolate-colored dogs) completely surrounded by rust-colored hairs, is a way of keeping the Toy Manchester, which requires this marking, out of the breed. Breeders say the thumb mark is either very dark and extensive, or blotchy and faded.

The disqualification for white exceeding one-half inch on any part of the dog is a curious one in that the standard permits white to exist so long as it does not exceed that measurement. The historical study of the Min Pin's origins reveals crossing with various terrier varieties, the Italian Greyhound and possibly others to establish the breed. Many of these earlier breeds had white coloration of one degree or another. It would appear that the desire to disqualify any dog with over half an inch of white is an effort on the part of a club consensus to try to keep the white coloration from becoming a dominant factor in the breed. Yet, one has to wonder why white is allowed to the small degree that it is as the white color, if permitted, can continue to be passed through a line.

All other colors not mentioned are also disqualifications as earlier colors have been phased out of existence with the breed becoming more refined and established as an individual entity.

8

Illustrated Standard

WORDS ARE SELDOM SUFFICIENT when trying to describe an animate object. A breed standard, which was designed by the parent club to serve as a blueprint for the breed, uses words as a guide to breed interpretation. The written words are important to everyone involved in the breed as they become the byways for understanding a particular breed. All breeders, exhibitors, handlers, judges—and even pet owners—should be fully cognizant of their dog's breed standard and apply this knowledge whether they are engaged in buying dogs for personal ownership, selecting breeding partners, establishing a show career or evaluating the animals in the ring. No standard should ever be taken lightly.

It is not just a standard's words that need emphasizing—it is the comprehension of those words that holds the key to the future of the breed. A mental picture must be firmly established of just what a breed is all about. Both negative and positive points of an animal must be evaluated as a dog is mentally measured against his breed standard. One of the best ways to develop a clearer understanding of this necessary mental picture is by studying illustrations of the breed. Illustrations permit a license in the mind of the creator in establishing similar, but different, traits and characteristics. For example, the artist can draw the same head with different ear lengths or the same basic body in which there are versions demonstrating level, sloping and dipping toplines. This creative license permits a viewer to visualize what happens to the overall picture as it is modified.

The illustrated standard is definitely one of the most helpful tools to use in comprehending a breed. Jacqueline Adams, a talented animal artist, has carefully prepared these accompanying illustrations to help us better understand the Miniature Pinscher.

A properly balanced Miniature Pinscher with slight arch to the neck and level topline.
All drawings by Jacqueline

Sloping topline.

Coarse, chunky body.

Short legs with too much body.

Long, shelly body; coarse muzzle lacking in underjaw.

High in rear.

A proper Min Pin head.

Long head with narrow topskull.

A coarse head with short muzzle and ears.

Wide, lowset ear placement.

Small, piercing eyes.

Incorrect, round eyes.

Pleasing eyes and cropped ears that are proportioned to the size and shape of the head.

Natural ears.

Exaggerated, long tapering ears.

Ears cropped too short.

Straight, upstanding front.

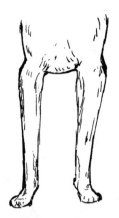

Fiddle front.

Out at the elbows.

Straight, parallel rear.

Weak, cowhocked rear.

Strong, well arched toes.

Flat, open feet.

Hackney-like gait with bend at the wrist or pasterns and good drive from the rear.

Hackney-like gait with no rear drive.

Goosestep, devoid of wrist bend, with good rear drive.

Straight front, crossing rear.

101

Two Canadian champions demonstrate the different breed types usually associated with the two main colors: black and rust, and red or stag.

9

Colors

ANOTHER FACTOR that a breeder needs to consider when deciding which dogs to select for matings is color. The present American Miniature Pinscher standard, dated July 1980, permits the following colors:

Color—Solid clear red. Stag red (red with intermingling of black hairs). Black with sharply defined rust-red markings on cheeks, lips, lower jaw, throat, twin spots above eyes and chest, lower half of forelegs, inside of hind legs and vent region, lower portion of hocks and feet. Black pencil stripes on toes. Chocolate with rust-red markings the same as specified for blacks except brown pencil stripes on toes. In solid red and stag red a rich vibrant medium to dark shade is preferred.

Disqualifications: Any color other than listed. Thumb mark (patch of black hair surrounded by rust on the front of the foreleg between the foot and the wrist; on chocolates, the patch is chocolate hair). White on any part of the dog which exceeds one-half (½) inch in its longest dimension.

Color is important in the Miniature Pinscher because the breed standard lists specific disqualifications for every judge to consider. Breeders who have raised a beautiful, quality animal with erroneous or deficient markings know too well the heartbreak involved. Before a discussion of color in breeding can be considered, it is necessary to thoroughly understand an interpretation of what the American standard is saying. Sharon A. Krogh, judge and breeder of K-Roc Min Pins with husband David M. Krogh, president of the MPCA, offered her views on color interpretation for the spring 1987 issue of *The Pinscher Patter,* the official publication of the MPCA:

> Over the years I have told many people that I do not have a color preference when it comes to the Miniature Pinscher! And I think that is a true statement. It follows that the overall structure of the dog is of primary importance.
>
> I would like to discuss color as stated in our breed standard, and as I interpret that standard.
>
> **"Color**—solid clear red." That means anything from a very dark fawn to a deep mahogany red, as long as there are no dark guard hairs! There can be some "bisking" over the shoulder blades and down the side of the neck, below the base of the ear, also, near the vent region. Other than this "bisking" the dog is solid red or a shade thereof.
>
> "Stag red (red with intermingling of black hairs)." This red also varies in its shades, but always has black guard hairs, usually over the back like a saddle and along the side of the neck from the base of the ear downward. Most of the time the heads are a clear deep red. Personally, I would prefer that they were. Occasionally you will see a stag red with a head that is clear red on one side and stag on the other, to say the least this does not make for a pleasing expression.
>
> "Black with sharply defined rust-red markings on cheeks, lips, lower jaw, throat, twin spots above eyes and chest, lower half of forelegs, inside of hind legs and vent region, lower portion of hocks and feet. Black pencil stripes on toes." The standard does a good job of telling us the proper markings on black and rust. It forgets to mention that the rust may range from dark fawn to rich mahogany, and that the black should be inky black and lustrous. A common problem we see in black and rusts is double rosettes. In other words, there are two sets of twin spots on the chest, the second set just above the properly placed set. Dogs with this problem may or may not have pencil stripes on their toes, or the twin spots above their eyes. They could very easily have a thumb print on their pastern (wrist) joint. (See: thumb print, under disqualifications.) To a lay person who may or may not know what a thumb print is, I would advise that you seek out a Manchester Terrier. The thumb print is mandatory in the Manchester. A very easy description is an island of black hairs on the pastern joint surrounded by rust-red hairs. The thumb print must be

Portrait of a top-winning red, Ch. Sanbrook Silk Trader, owned by Ruth H. Norwood, bred by Ann Dutton.

A BIS-winning black and rust-red male owned by David and Sharon Krogh, bred by Ron Preston, was Ch. K-Roc's Two for a Penny.

An unusual and lovely chocolate with rust markings is Ch. Rei-Mar's Chip Off the Ol' Bloc, owned and bred by Rei-Mar Kennels.
Ross

105

an island, it is *not* an extension of the black hairs coming down the leg.

"Chocolate with rust-red markings the same as specified for blacks, except brown pencil stripes on toes." The markings will vary in shade according to the richness of the chocolate color. Worth mentioning is the following quote from the portion of the standard regarding the head: "*Eyes*—Full, slightly oval, clear, bright and dark even to a true black, including eye rims, with the exception of chocolates whose eye rims should be self-colored. *Nose*—Black only, with the exception of chocolates which should have a self-colored nose." The self-colored nose and eye rims have a tendency to leave the chocolate looking rather plain in the face.

"In the solid red and stag red a rich vibrant medium to dark shade is preferred." I believe this was tucked in almost as an afterthought. This statement is important and probably should have included the blacks and chocolates as far as the words "rich and vibrant" are concerned.

"*Disqualifications:* Any color other than listed. Thumb mark (patch of black hair surrounded by rust on the front of the foreleg between the foot and the wrist; on chocolates, the patch is chocolate hair). White on any part of the dog which exceeds one-half (½) in its longest dimension." The original interpretation from the German breed standard dated 1929, quoted in part: "Color B. Solid yellow; C. Blue or blue-toned with red or yellow markings; D. Spotted on white body, flecked, mostly grey, with black spots and red or yellow markings." It was not until our standard dated 1950 that these two colors became faults. And, not until the standard of 1980 did they become a disqualification. The final reference to color in the current standard is the white that is not to exceed one-half inch in its longest dimension. That is pretty plain!

So, what color the Min-Pin? They may be red, stag-red, black and rust or chocolate. All judged equally, as long as their color conforms to the breed standard. I have no color preferences, but I do prefer a structurally sound animal!

10

Color Genetics

IN THE UNITED STATES Miniature Pinscher color-
ing is important because there are color and marking disqualifications listed in the breed's standard. With the increased acceptance of
uncropped ears among American show dogs and the potential for
importation of dogs from those countries that do not crop ears and
permit colors other than those listed in the United States (for
instance, England permits blue with tan markings), it is necessary
for breeders contemplating the importation of foreign dogs to have a
thorough understanding of not only pedigrees and the American
standard, but also the effects of color genetics in a breeding
program. William Ledbetter, an American who resides in Germany,
where color is a prime consideration in all breeds, has prepared the
following study of color genetics in the Miniature Pinscher. Much of
his research is based on the book *The Inheritance of Coat Color in
Dogs,* by Clarence C. Little (Howell 1957).

I.   **The Forms of Gene A:**
      a^y Restricts the area of dark hair pigment and produces
             the color solid clear red in Miniature Pinschers; the
             strength of this gene determines darker or lighter
             shades of red.

Red, or stag red, is the predominant color in America. *Candids by Connie*

Although black with rust markings is the predominant color combination in Germany, hence the prevailing Continental type in that color, America's black and rusts can also be sleek and refined. *Candids by Connie*

a^t Produces black with rust-red markings (black and tan) in Miniature Pinschers; this gene can be covered up by the gene a^y for red. In other words, the gene a^y is dominant over a^t for black and rust in Miniature Pinschers. The gene a^y for clear solid red may be strengthened by the simultaneous presence of a^t to produce deeper, intense red or stag red (red with intermingling of black hairs).

II. The Forms of Gene B:

B   Produces black pigmentation of nose, foot-pads and eye-rims; produces black pigment granules in both the inner and outer layers of each hair strand.

b   Produces brown or chocolate pigmentation of nose and eye-rims; restricts the pigment formation in the hair to chocolate or lighter reddish-brown shades.

III. The Forms of Gene C:

C   The gene for full depth of pigmentation; produces a deep, rich intensity of red, chocolate or black hair coloring. Other forms of gene C are not accepted by the standard.

IV. The Forms of Gene D:

D   Regulates a heavy deposit of all pigment granules in each hair strand.

d   Dilutes the black pigmentation in blues (for example, in the blue Doberman Pinscher); or the dilute chocolate pigmentation as seen in the fawn-colored Doberman Pinscher and Weimaraners. In recent years, this gene has been proven to be linked with many skin diseases, as well as neurological defects; this gene is fortunately no longer accepted by the Miniature Pinscher standard in the United States and in Germany.

V. The Forms of Gene E:

E   Allows the formation of black, chocolate or dark pigment in each hair strand. Other forms of gene E are not accepted by the standard.

VI. The Forms of Gene G:

G   Changes a puppy's coat, which is at birth of a uniform dark color, later in the direction of increasing grayness or pale shading; this gene is not accepted by the Min Pin standard.

g   Constant pigmentation.

VII. The Forms of Gene M:

M   Produces harlequins (merles), which were formerly accepted by the standard in the United States and in Germany, but are now excluded; often one or both eyes were light blue or had variegated pigmentation. If a dog inherited this gene from both parents, he was usually deaf, blind and sterile.

m   Uniform pigmentation.

VIII. The Forms of Gene P:

P   Normal pigmentation formation.

p   Reduces black pigmentation to "lilac" and chocolate to light yellowish fawn; this gene is not accepted by the Min Pin standard.

IX. The Forms of Gene S:

S   Solid-colored coat with no spots of white on toes or chest.

s^p Parti-colored (spotted) dogs; not accepted by the Min Pin standard.

X. The Forms of Gene T:

T   Flecks or "ticking" in light areas; not accepted by Min Pin standard.

t   Clear, unticked coat.

Using the above symbols and the symbol x for any other gene form of the letter to the left of the symbol x:

BLACK AND TAN (BLACK AND RUST-RED) MIN PINS:
$a^t a^t$ Bx   Cx   Dx   Sx   gg   mm   Px   tt

HARLEQUIN MIN PINS (formerly accepted, but no longer accepted by the breed standard:
$a^t a^t$ Bx   Cx   Dx   Ex   Sx   gg   Mx   Px   tt

RED MIN PINS (clear solid red):
Type 1: $a^y a^y$ Bx   Cx   Dx   Ex   SX   gg   mm
           Px   tt

Type 2: $a^y a^t$ Bx   Cx   Dx   Ex   Sx   gg   mm
           Px   tt

Clear, solid red may be Type 1 or Type 2; stag red (red with intermingling of black hairs) may be produced by a very strong gene a^y or the interaction of a^y with a simultaneously present a^t. The latter is the most frequent explanation for stag red.

CHOCOLATE MIN PINS WITH RUST-RED MARKINGS:
$a^t a^t$ bb   Cx   Dx   Ex   Sx   gg   mm   Px   tt

BROWN-NOSED (LIVER-NOSED) RED MIN PINS (excluded from the standard):
$a^y a^y$ bb   Cx   Dx   Ex   Sx   gg   mm   Px   tt

OR

$a^y a^t$ bb   Cx   Dx   Ex   Sx   gg   mm   Px   tt

A mating of two black and rust-red Min Pins

$$a^ta^t \quad BB \quad x \quad a^ta^t \quad BB$$

can only produce black and rust-red pups, unless both dogs mated carried the gene b:

$$a^ta^t \quad Bb \quad x \quad a^ta^t \quad Bb$$

This would allow that one pup out of four (according to the law of averages) would be chocolate with rust-red markings: $a^ta^t \quad bb$.

A mating of a black and rust-red Min Pin and a clear solid red

$$a^ta^t \quad x \quad a^ya^y$$

would produce a litter of red or stag red pups; however, if the red parent carried the gene for black and rust-red (a^ya^t), then this dog, when mated with a black and rust-red dog, would produce a litter in which half of the pups would be red or stag red and the other half would be black and rust-red (according to the law of averages).

The mating of two chocolate Min Pins with rust-red markings

$$a^ta^t \quad bb \quad x \quad a^ta^t \quad bb$$

can only produce pups of this chocolate color with rust-red markings.

The mating of two reds or stag reds of the type

$$a^ya^t \quad x \quad a^ya^t$$

whereby both dogs carry the gene for black and rust-red (a^t), would produce a litter in which approximately one black and rust-red pup to three red or stag red pups could be expected (according to the law of averages).

The mating of a chocolate Min Pin with rust-red markings to a black and rust-red would produce a litter in which all pups would be black and rust-red, unless the black and rust-red dog carried the gene for chocolate with rust-red markings (b); in this case, one half of the pups would be chocolate with rust-red markings, the other half of the pups would be black and rust-red (according to the law of averages).

After completing this study, Mr. Ledbetter spoke with Mrs. Erna Lang, a prominent German Min Pin breeder of reds, stag reds and blacks with rust-red markings. She offered the following input based on her experiences:

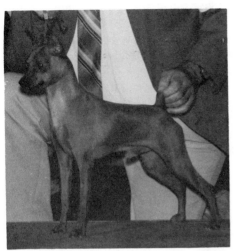

Group winner, Ch. K-Roc's Burning Gold, bred and owned by David and Sharon Krogh, Oregon.
Lindemaier

Group winner, Ch. King-Pins Jitterbug, bred by King Pin, Linda Kazan Stevens and W.L. Aston, owned by Marion J. Gutierrz, Kentucky.
Petrulis

Ch. Ben-Lyn's Southern Song, bred and owned by Vickie L. Jones, West Virginia. *Booth*

Group winner, Ch. Blythewood Ain't I Something, bred and owned by Joan L. Huber, Pennsylvania.
Klein

113

If a bitch tends to bear dilute red pups, always breed it thereafter to a black and rust-red male. This will give the offspring a very intense, bright red or stag red.

If, however, a black and rust-red bitch tends to bear pups with too much black or with incorrect rust-red markings, breed this bitch from then on to a red (or stag red) stud. The pups will then almost always have the correct coloring of red, or black and rust, depending on the stud.

If a red or stag red bitch has a black and rust-red parent, breeding the bitch to a black and rust-red stud should give 50% red or stag red pups, and 50% black and rust-red pups.

Mrs. Lang reported that she has occasionally bred two stag reds together, both of which had a black and rust-red parent, and received a litter of five to six pups—one or two being black and rust-red, although both parents were stag reds. This confirms the fact that black and rust-red is recessive to the dominant color red in Miniature Pinschers.

Mrs. Lang further said that if a bitch were derived from a long line of red to red breeding, then the bitch, when bred to a black and rust-red stud, would produce in most cases nothing but red or stag red pups. This is another confirmation that red is dominant (epistatic) to black and rust-red. As Bill Ledbetter explains, "The gene a^y (red) covers up the gene a^t (black and rust-red); however the interaction of the a^t with a^y tends to produce a very intense red or stag red, usually with an intermingling of some black hair strands."

Breeders who are serious about the potential of color genetics would be interested in a study done by Mrs. Elfriede Paech of West Germany. Mrs. Paech is a breeder of the Old German Standard Pinscher, which is the larger and older variety of the Miniature Pinscher in Germany. The Old German Standard Pinscher and the Miniature Pinscher share the same standard, with the only difference being size requirements. Mrs. Paech tabulated this study from the records in the German Standard Pinscher Registry of the German Pinscher-Schnauzer Klub for the years 1967 to 1985:

114

63 litters where both parents were red
   (or stag)   =   16.5%

52 litters where the sire was black/rust-red,
   the dam was another color   =   13.6%

1 litter where the sire was blue/rust-red,
   the dam was another color   =   0.3%

62 litters where the sire was red (or stag),
   the dam was another color   =   16.3%

62 litters where the dam was black/rust-red,
   the sire was another color   =   16.3%

2 litters where the dam was blue/rust-red,
   the sire was another color   =   0.5%

51 litters where the dam was red (or stag),
   the sire was another color   =   13.5%

Of the 1,807 puppies:

1,191 were black/rust-red	=	65.9%
583 were red (or stag)	=	32.3%
26 were blue/rust-red	=	1.4%
5 were bronze-colored		
1 was isabella (fawn)		
1 was chocolate/rust-red		
These last 7	=	0.4%

Of 928 pups, both of whose parents were black/rust-red:

900 were black/rust-red	=	97.0%
18 were blue/rust-red	=	1.9%
9 were red (or stag)	=	1.0%
1 was chocolate/rust-red	=	0.1%

From 381 Min Pin litters (yielding 1,807 pups) during the years 1967 through 1985 there were:

203 litters where both parents were black/
   rust-red   =   53.3%

(One can readily determine here that gene b for chocolate and gene d for fawn and blue are definitely recessive color-dilution genes, covered up by the dominant genes B for black pigmentation of nose, eye-rims and/or hair of the coat and gene D for normal pigment intensity and distribution in the black/rust-red parent animals bred.)

Of 306 pups, both of whose parents were red (or stag):

34 were black/rust-red	=	11.1%
3 were blue/rust-red	=	1.0%
266 were red (or stag)	=	86.9%
2 were bronze-colored	=	0.7%
1 was isabella (fawn)	=	0.3%

(Here one can readily see that gene a^y for red is dominant over gene a^t for black/rust-red, since black/rust-red pups appeared in litters of red sire and dam. In addition, one can also see that the recessive gene d for blue and isabella (fawn) pups was covered up by the dominant gene D in the parent dogs with normal red (or stag) pigment distribution and intensity.)

Of 568 pups resulting in breedings in which one parent was black/rust-red and the other parent red (or stag):

251 pups were black/rust-red	=	44.0%
6 were blue/rust-red	=	1.2%
308 were red (or stag)	=	54.2%
3 were isabella (fawn)	=	0.5%

(The ratio 251:308, which approximates 1:1, shows that in almost every case the red parent was carrying, in addition to gene a^y for red, also a gene for black/rust-red ($a^y a^t$), and that breeders were breeding for pups of both colors in the anticipated litters. Again we can readily observe that gene d for blue or isabella (fawn) was a rare recessive gene that appears quite unexpectedly in a very small number of pups, since it must be inherited from both parent dogs in order to manifest itself.)

Bill Ledbetter, who translated this material from German into English, added the comments that appear in parentheses. He also

116

stated that blue or fawn (isabella) parent dogs are no longer used for breeding in Germany, as that country disallowed those colors in 1984.

Color is an important consideration in any breeding program where specific colors, or color combinations, are exempted by virtue of the breed's standard. However, all colors that come within the standard should be considered equally when one is attesting to overall quality and color becomes just another consideration. As Sharon Krogh emphasized in her interpretative view of the standard's permitted colors, structural soundness also needs studying by any breeder when contemplating a breeding program. No dog ever should be bred or shown purely because of its color. Potential breeders and exhibitors must also review the animal's structure, condition and temperament and make a judgment based on all the positive and negative features of the animal(s) involved.

Min Pins love everyone and strongly advocate people contact. A close look at this photograph from Germany reveals one of Erna Lang's Min Pins perched on top of the shoulders of Mr. Lang, while another rests between his back and the chair.

11

Standard Comparisons

WITH TODAY'S JET-AGE, where breeders can easily import and export dogs, it is important to not only understand color, but also to know the different standards that exist around the world and realize how those standards may affect any breeding program. Three particular Min Pin standards—United States, Great Britain, and Federation Cynologique Internationale—have been chosen for comparison purposes. The FCI is a federation of national kennel clubs from around the world and its breed standards are usually those of the respective breed's country of origin. In this case, the Min Pin's country of origin is considered to be Germany. The FCI standard was translated by William Ledbetter.

General Appearance

US—The Miniature Pinscher is structurally a well-balanced, sturdy, compact, short-coupled, smooth-coated dog. He naturally is well groomed, proud, vigorous and alert. Characteristic traits are his hackney-like action, fearless animation, complete self-possession, and his spirited presence.

GB—Well-balanced, sturdy, compact, elegant, short-coupled, smooth-coated toy dog. Naturally well groomed, proud, vigorous and alert. *Characteristics:* Precise hackney gait, fearless animation, complete self-possession and spirited presence. *Temperament:* Fearless and alert.

FCI—The Pinscher is smooth-coated, streamlined and fluent in contour, with well-proportioned symmetry and well-balanced harmony in the entire body form, but robust with well-distributed muscle formation and a quadratic, short-coupled, compact body build. The Pinscher must trot, not pace, in diagonal sequence. In temperament, the Pinscher is spirited, energetic, attentive, alert, watchful; in character, the Pinscher is good natured, attached and devoted to his master, with an incorruptible, unbribable guard instinct without being a nerve-racking, yapping barker. Because the Pinscher is short-haired and smooth-coated, he is easy to keep in the apartment or home. Highly developed sense organs, intelligence, obedience, trainability, fearlessness, endurance and resistance to diseases give the Pinscher all the prerequisites for being a superb watchdog and companion.

The Miniature Pinscher is the exact replica in miniature of the Old German Standard Pinscher. The Miniature Pinscher must show none of the shortcomings and faults commonly found in other toy breeds. The temperament of the Miniature Pinscher corresponds also to that of the Old German Standard Pinscher, perhaps even more animated and spirited. Vigorous and alert, the Miniature Pinscher fulfills all the duties of a larger watchdog; as a smooth-coated toy, the Miniature Pinscher is easy to keep in the smallest apartment or house. Except for the smaller size, the Standard of the Miniature Pinscher is the same as that of the Old German Standard Pinscher.

Head

US—In correct proportion to the body. Tapering, narrow with well-fitted but not too prominent foreface which balances with the skull. No indication of coarseness. *Skull:* Appears flat, tapering forward toward the muzzle. *Muzzle:* Strong rather than fine and delicate, and in proportion to the head as a whole. Head well-balanced with only a slight drop to the muzzle, which is parallel to the top of the skull. *Nose:* Black only, with the exception of chocolates which should have a self-colored nose. *Teeth:* Meet in a

119

scissors bite. *Eyes:* Full, slightly oval, clear, bright and dark even to a true black, including eye rims, with the exception of chocolates, whose eye rims should be self-colored. *Ears:* Set high, standing erect from base to top. May be cropped or uncropped. *Lips and Cheeks:* Small, taut and closely adherent to each other.

GB—More elongated than short and round. Narrow, without conspicuous cheek formation. In proportion to body. Skull flat when viewed from front. Muzzle rather strong and proportionate to skull. Nostrils well formed. Nose black with the exception of chocolate and blue in which it may be self-colored. *Eyes:* Fitting well into face. Neither too full nor round, nor too small or slanting. Black or nearly black. *Ears:* Set on high, as small as possible, erect or dropped. *Mouth:* Jaws strong, with a perfect, regular and complete scissors bite, i.e., the upper teeth closely overlapping the lower teeth and set square to the jaws.

FCI—The head is strong and elongated, without having a pronounced occiput. The overall length (tip of the nose to the occiput) and length of back (from the withers to tail) should be 1:2 in ratio. The bridge of the nose, running parallel to a line extrapolated from the unwrinkled, smooth, flat forehead, possesses a very slight but distinct stop. The jaw musculature must be strong, but the cheeks should not be prominent. The deep muzzle ends in a blunt wedge. The nose is full and black. The chocolates with red markings must have dark brown pigmentation of nose and eye-rims. *Bite:* The scissors bite, whereby the incisors of the upper jaw reach slightly over the incisors of the lower jaw, should be complete. The teeth must be pure, sparkling white. *Ears:* Dogs with cropped ears, whelped before January 1, 1987, must have uniformly cropped ears, set high and held erect. Uncropped dogs have V-shaped ears folded down close to the head or ears must be small and erect whereby both ears must be held uniformly erect. (In Germany, up until January 1, 1987, when ear cropping became legally disallowed, the ears were usually cropped; however, ear cropping was not a requirement. No dogs whelped after January 1, 1987 may be registered or shown in shows with cropped ears.) *Eyes:* Dark, medium sized, oval and

120

directed forward. The lower eyelids are tight, so that the conjunctiva are not visible.

Neck

US—Proportioned to head and body, slightly arched, gracefully curved, blending into shoulders, muscular and free from suggestion of dewlap or throatiness.

GB—Strong yet graceful, slightly arched. Well fitted into shoulders. Free from throatiness.

FCI—Strong with beautiful arch. Should be neither too short nor too thick. The skin around the throat is tight with no sags, wrinkles or folds.

Body

US—*Topline:* Back level or slightly sloping toward the rear both when standing and gaiting. Length of males equals height at withers. Females may be slightly longer. *Chest and Ribs:* Body compact, slightly wedge-shaped, muscular with well-sprung ribs. Depth of brisket, the base line of which is level with points of the elbows. *Loin:* Short and strong in loin with belly moderately tucked up to denote grace of structural form. *Croup:* Level with topline.

GB—Square, back line straight, sloping slightly towards rear. Belly moderately tucked up. Ribs well sprung, deep rather than barrelled. Viewed from top slightly wedge shaped.

FCI—Chest is moderately wide with flat ribs and oval cross-section. Brisket extends to the elbows. The forechest is formed by the sternum, which extends beyond the joint of the shoulder blade and upper arm. The underbody rises gradually towards the rear with a moderate tuck up at the loin. The short distance from the last pair of ribs to the hip bone gives the dog a compact appearance. The total length of the body is approximately the same as the height at the withers. The back is short and slightly sloping. The topline is not straight, but shows a very slight curve from the strong, first vertebra of the withers, over the back to a slightly rounded croup and base of the tail.

121

Tail

US—Set high, held erect, docked in proportion to size of dog.

GB—Continuation of topline carried a little high and customarily docked short.

FCI—The tail set is high and is held erect. Must be docked to first three vertebral joints.

Forequarters

US—*Forechest:* Well-developed. *Shoulders:* Clean and sloping with moderate angulation coordinated to permit the hackney-like action. *Legs:* Strong bone development and small clean joints. As viewed from the front, straight and upstanding, elbows close to the body. *Pasterns:* Strong, perpendicular. *Feet:* Small, cat-like, toes strong, well arched and closely knit with deep pads. *Nails:* Thick, blunt. *Dewclaws:* Should be removed from both front and hind legs.

GB—Forechest well developed and full, moderately broad; shoulders clean, sloping with moderate angulation. Legs straight, medium bone, elbows close to body. *Feet:* Cat-like feet; nails dark.

FCI—Slanted shoulder blades and upper arms are well angulated and flat, but well muscled. Forelegs are straight when viewed from the side. Elbows close to the body. *Feet:* Small, round and closely knit, arched toes (cat-like paws) with dark toenails and tough, hard pads.

Hindquarters

US—Well-muscled quarters set wide enough apart to fit into a properly balanced body. As viewed from the rear, the legs are straight and parallel. From the side, well-angulated. *Thighs:* Well-muscled. *Stifles:* Well defined. *Hocks:* Short, set well apart.

GB—Parallel and wide enough apart to fit in with a properly built body. Hindquarters well developed, muscular with good sweep of stifle, and hocks turning neither in nor out. Legs straight, medium bone.

FCI—Well-angulated and well-muscled. Hocks must not turn inward becoming cow-hocked.

Movement

US—The forelegs and hindlegs move parallel, with feet turning neither in nor out. The hackney-like action is a high-stepping, reaching, free and easy gait in which the front leg moves straight forward and in front of the body and the foot bends at the wrist. The dog drives smoothly and strongly from the rear. The head and tail are carried high.

GB—Co-ordinated to permit a true hackneyed action.

FCI—The Pinscher must trot, not pace, in diagonal sequence.

Coat

US—Smooth, hard and short, straight and lustrous, closely adhering to and uniformly covering the body.

GB—Smooth, hard and short. Straight and lustrous. Closely adhering to and uniformly covering body. Hair forming ridge on any part of head, body or legs highly undesirable.

FCI—Smooth, short, dense and lustrous, closely adhering to the body without any bald spots.

Color

US—Solid clear red. Stag red (red with intermingling of black hairs). Black with sharply defined rust-red markings on cheeks, lips, lower jaw, throat, twin spots above eyes and chest, lower half of forelegs, inside of hindlegs and vent region, lower portion of hocks and feet. Black pencil stripes on toes. Chocolates with rust-red markings the same as specified for blacks, except brown pencil stripes on toes. In the solid red and stag red a rich vibrant medium to dark shade is preferred. *Disqualifications:* Any color other than listed. Thumb mark (patch of black hair surrounded by rust on the front of the foreleg between the foot and the wrist; on chocolates, the patch is chocolate hair). White on any part of dog which exceeds one-half (½) inch in its longest dimension.

GB—Black, blue, chocolate with sharply defined tan markings on cheeks, lips, lower jaw, throat, twin spots above eyes and chest, lower half of forelegs, inside of hindlegs and vent region, lower portion of hocks and feet. All above colours have black pencilling on toes without thumb marks. Solid red of various shades. Slight white on chest permissible but undesirable.

FCI—Solid red in various shades to stag red; or black, or even chocolate, with red or rust-red markings. Dark, rich, sharply defined markings are desirable. The markings are evenly distributed as follows: at the cheeks, lips, lower jaw, above both eyes, at the throat, on the sternum as two triangular-shaped twin spots, on the lower half of the forelegs, the feet, inside the hindlegs and the vent region.

Size

US—Ten (10) inches to twelve and one-half (12½) inches in height allowed, with desired height eleven (11) inches to eleven and one-half (11½) inches measured at highest point of the shoulder blades. *Disqualification:* Under ten (10) inches or over twelve and one-half (12½) inches in height.

GB—Height from 25.5–30 cm. (10–12 inches) at withers.

FCI—Height measured at the withers if 43 to 48 cm. (17 to 19 inches) for the Old German Standard Pinscher; and for the Miniature Pinscher, the height is 25 to 30 cm. (10 to 12 inches).

12

Whelping and Raising a Litter

ARMED WITH A WEALTH of knowledge regarding standards, colors and bloodlines; tooled with a thorough understanding of the positive and negative aspects of a potential brood bitch; and satisfied as to the possible benefits of a mating with a particular stud dog and his bloodlines to that bitch—a breeder is ready to embark on the path of breeding quality Min Pins.

Whelping and raising a litter of puppies is not easy. Not only is it necessary to be versed in matters of mating, equipped with proper facilities and braced against an unknown that is bound to happen, a breeder-to-be must also be hardened to endure swings of emotion— extreme joy when a pup is born and heartbreaking sadness if it dies. There are many excellent books available covering the subjects of breeding, whelping and raising puppies. Every person who desires to undertake such a journey should buy those books and read them from cover to cover and over again until the important chapters are known by heart. It is also advisable to seek the assistance and advice of a local breeder and have contact with an experienced veterinarian who is knowledgeable about handling small dogs.

Breeding a bitch to a stud dog should never be a sudden occasion. It is necessary to plan well in advance of the breeding. It is vital to take the time to carefully assess the entire situation, make

A beautiful Min Pin is any breeder's reward. Ch. Fillpin's Hot Toddy, owned by Judy Fillpot, Fillpin Kennels.
Graham

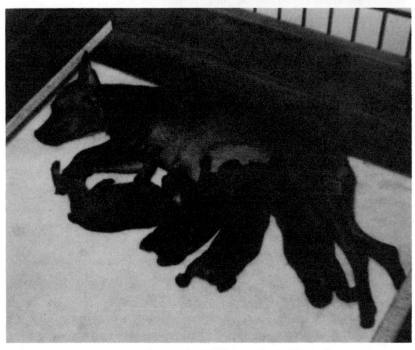

A Canadian litter owned by Gerona E. MacCuaig.

early contacts, ascertain the availability of the complementary stud, be sure of the health of both dogs, appraise the veterinarian should assistance be needed and, in short, preplan and prepare anything and everything in order to assure a successful whelping and a healthy, happy dam and babies.

The best way to learn about whelping and raising puppies is to talk with other breeders. Min Pins are small dogs and as such may require special care. One prominent breeder, Judy Fillpot of Fillpin Kennels in Iowa, passes along some of her techniques:

Well before whelping time make sure contact has been made with an experienced, trusted veterinarian. About a week before puppies are due, I like to check with the vet to alert him that whelping is imminent, and to learn exactly who will be on call nights and weekends in case of difficulties.

About a week before due date, I begin to check the bitch's temperature so that I can learn what is normal for her, usually about 101.5°. Thereafter, I check the temperature if the bitch is to be left alone, or if she seems nervous. If the temperature has dropped below 100° (usually it will go down to 98° or 99°), labor generally begins within eight hours and the bitch should be carefully watched.

The room for whelping should be warm—around 78°. A puppy pen that is about waist high on the whelper is helpful and may be either commercially manufactured or self-made. This makes both bitch and puppies easier to work with, plus gets them off the floor and away from drafts. The bottom half of an airline crate filled with newspaper works well as a whelping box. The plastic can be scrubbed for sanitation and wet, dirty paper is easily replaced. Also, just before the onset of labor, as well as during it, most bitches will scratch, tear and bite at their bedding to prepare a nest. This activity seems to help them speed up labor and the newspaper provides good material for nesting.

During whelping, I always cut the cord, as the dam may pull on it or chew it too close to the puppy's body causing a hernia or abdominal wound. Then I remove the puppy from the sack, and sling it to remove mucus from the air passages. The slinging is done this way: wrap the puppy in a rough towel (puppies are slippery). Turn it until its back is toward the floor; carefully support the head, neck and back with one hand, and hold on tightly with the other hand. Lift the puppy high above your head and sling it toward the floor with a good pop at the

Two proud littermates who later became Canadian Best in Show winners for Gerona MacCuaig.

Another foursome, this time from the MacCuaigs in Canada.

A unique hideaway for these four pups owned by the Towells, Australia.

A black and rust collection from Erna Lang, West Germany.

A black and rust surveying the vast green world around him. Angelika Grabellus, West Germany.

129

end, being sure again that the head is braced so that you do not break its neck. This will clear the air passages, but extra care must be taken not to drop the puppy. This procedure also works if a puppy chokes on milk.

As each puppy after the first is about to be born, remove the others to a small box warmed with a hot water bottle or heating pad. This allows the bitch to concentrate on the current birth without being distracted by stepping or sitting on the others and hearing them cry.

When whelping seems to be complete, take the bitch outside to relieve herself. Then bring her in and give her a bowl of broth. While she eats, place into her box fresh paper covered with a towel or other slightly rough fabric so that the puppies can have traction for nursing. Be careful not to use so much cloth that the puppies can get buried and possibly squashed by the bitch.

When all is clean, settle the bitch back into her box with her whelps and make sure that each nurses a good meal of the colostrum that is produced at first and is so important in giving immunity to the puppies. Continue to watch the bitch for an hour or two in case you only thought she was finished and she produces another puppy. Within 12 hours of whelping, take the bitch to the vet for a "pit" shot. This will clear out any retained placenta material, and allows the vet to check the puppies for such defects as a minute cleft palate that you might have missed.

For the next few days, continue to add broth to the high-quality commercial puppy food that the bitch was fed during pregnancy. This extra liquid helps in milk production and rehydration of the bitch's body after the rigors of whelping. Be careful to continue giving the vitamin/mineral (with special emphasis on calcium and phosphorous) supplement that your vet recommended for pregnancy throughout the lactation period to prevent eclampsia, a convulsive paralysis caused by calcium deficiency in the bitch. Increase the amount of food as the bitch's appetite demands, and also increase the number of meals per day to three or four to reduce the amount that she will want to eat at a time.

Problems in whelping? The answer is usually to call the vet. A few instances to be on the alert for:

If the bitch labors in the beginning more than two or three hours without producing a puppy;

If the interval between puppies' birth is more than one hour;

If any puppy weighs less than 3 oz., you will need proper instructions and equipment for tube feeding. Do not hesitate to supplement with the tube method if a puppy loses weight or appears dehydrated. Check for dehydration by gently pinching the skin. Upon release, the skin of a healthy puppy will spring back to smooth. If dehydrated, the skin will remain pinched. Again, for procedure and amount, follow the vet's instructions, and don't give up as long as there is life. You just might be saving the best Min Pin you ever bred.

Also consult the vet if the bitch shows signs of eclampsia, such as severe trembling, jerking or convulsions.

RAISING PUPPIES

During the first week or two of life, keep puppies warm—78° to 80°—and run a humidifier in the room to provide moisture. This helps their breathing and prevents skin from drying out.

At three or five days of age, the tails are docked. However, if a puppy is weak or got a bad start, wait a few more days until it is stable and thriving.

The ears are cropped later. Some breeders have them done when the pup reaches three pounds in weight. I personally wait until 16 weeks of age, as this allows each puppy to have completed its series of inoculations, plus attaining some semblance of its adult appearance. Ear cropping is tricky, and should be done by someone with experience as a poor crop can ruin the appearance of an otherwise well-conformed Min Pin. The long, slender ear crop now in vogue generally requires some type of bracing after cutting to assure a straight, high stand. Follow the advice of the vet or the bitch's breeder on this point, as they will know what will work best for specific ear types.

At or before birth, learn your vet's recommended inoculation schedule and follow it faithfully. Your investment in time, money and affection can be rapidly gone if parvo or distemper strikes unprotected puppies.

When puppies' eyes are open and they are walking well, it's time to teach them to eat from a dish. Use the high-quality commercial puppy food you are already feeding the bitch. Place a small amount of it in the blender with some warm water, reduce it to a thin slush and pour it into a shallow dish or pan. Place the puppies, one at a time, at the food, dipping their mouths into it. They quickly get the hang of eating and soon begin to get more on the inside than the outside. Keep an eye out to be sure each puppy gets its share.

At one month of age the puppies should be eating well on their own, four meals a day, and the time has come to begin weaning them. The bitch is likely to be tired of them and will be happy to cooperate.

131

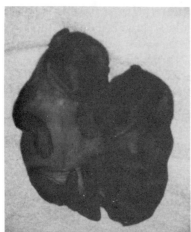

Phalen's week-old female pups.

.Natural eared Mom and her two babies. Owned by the Towells, Australia.

A foursome for Lindy and Buddy Stevens, Kentucky.

At first, she should be removed from the puppies for two or three daytime hours while still allowed to sleep with them at night. Gradually lengthen the time apart until by six to eight weeks of age, the puppies are completely on their own.

The puppies should continue to sleep in the crate, and its cover should be added after they are weaned. As soon as they stop having to go outside the crate at night to relieve themselves, the crate door should be closed. Thus, you will have crate-trained puppies, which will be most helpful whether they are destined to be show dogs or pets.

This crate training will be useful in their house training. As soon as they crawl, they will leave their box to relieve themselves. Surround the box with newspaper so they will begin learning to "use the paper." As they grow older, move the box to a larger, enclosed space, still covered with paper. Gradually decrease the amount of floor space covered with paper, until only one fairly small area is left covered. With luck, most of the puppies will follow the paper. If they miss, try to catch them at it and quickly move them to the paper, encouraging them to go there. This early paper training is helpful, particularly for show dogs or pets that cannot always be exercised outdoors.

As soon as first inoculations are given, expose the puppies to as many different people and situations as possible to socialize them and prevent kennel-shy dogs. Spend as much time with them yourself as possible, playing with them and getting to know them as individuals. This is not only good for them in causing emotional bonding with humans, but will also help you in deciding which should go to show or pet homes, and which you may want to keep. Don't forget to enjoy them as puppies for they grow up too fast.

13

Tails and Dewclaws

MINIATURE PINSCHERS ARE naturally a long-tailed breed. If their tails were left undocked, the length and shape would be similar to that of the Manchester Terrier. Docking the tail to a shorter length has been a long-accepted practice in Min Pins and breeders have this done when the puppies are just a few days old.

Another early minor surgery that must be attended to is the removal of any dewclaws that might exist on the front and hind legs of the newborn pups. The dewclaws are sometimes referred to as "fifth" toes and are the thumb-like appendages that, if present, appear on the inside of the legs. They are unnecessary and unprotected in a Min Pin, and if left on may catch and be torn off in later years. If removed when the pup is young, the pain is slight.

A veterinarian who has had a lot of experience with removing dewclaws and docking tails is William C. Harris, DVM, Salem, Wisconsin. He recommends the following:

> Dewclaw removal and tail docking of young puppies can be a fast and minor procedure. If certain guidelines are followed, any complications should be minimal. If these guidelines are not followed, complications can and do occur, such as excessive unsightly scar tissue, regrowth of dewclaws, infection and stress to the puppies.
>
> The first and most important thing is the puppy's age. Puppies should be done no sooner than two to three days old and no older than five to seven days. I feel it is important to wait at least two or three

days to make sure the puppy is sucking and able to withstand the stress. Any weak puppy should be nursed along before surgery. It is important not to wait any longer than seven days, as this minor procedure can become a major surgery.

Both procedures can be accomplished with the following sterile supplies: an eight-inch kelly forceps, a six-inch mosquito forceps, a needle, a needle holder, an absorbable suture, seven percent iodine and a clotting solution or powder, if needed.

Dewclaws are done first. The puppy is alcohol-swabbed, and with a six-inch mosquito forceps, the dewclaw is clamped under the second joint. In many cases, the closure of the clamp itself will cut the toe. To facilitate removal, the surgeon's thumbnail is scratched along the forceps. The clamp is removed and the area iodined. Any bleeding can be controlled with a stitch or with clotting powder.

The tails are done next. First a measurement for proper length is made. Most measuring charts are based on puppies less than one week of age. The tail is cleaned with alcohol and a kelly forceps is clamped in place. The excess tail is twisted rather than cut off. An absorbable suture is placed in the tail to close the skin, and then it is dipped in iodine. Clotting solution can be used if necessary.

Puppies should be checked for bleeding and returned to the mother. The mother and puppies should be kept in a clean environment. The mother will keep the puppies clean; if needed, use three percent peroxide twice daily on tails and dewclaws.

One of the biggest problems with docking tails is the chance of either cutting too much or too little. The chart Dr. Harris refers to appears in Kirk's *Current Veterinary Therapy VI*. This chart, which was compiled by M. Josephine Deubler, VMD, suggests leaving ½ inch or two vertebrae for the Miniature Pinscher. Dr. Deubler states that this is an approximate guide for docking "when done before puppy is one week old." She also cautions: "An improperly docked tail may ruin a puppy for show purposes. If one is in doubt, consultation with an established breeder is suggested. There may be variations among puppies, and a knowledge of breed characteristics is important in determining the correct length to dock."

Judy Fillpot, Fillpin Kennels, recommends: "One rule of thumb for docking is to leave ⅜″ attached." She also admonishes owners to "watch puppies carefully for an hour or two after the surgery to be sure there is no bleeding, or that the mother does not overly lick and worry the stump."

No novice or amateur should ever attempt to dock tails. An improper dock that does not correctly heal can lead to infection and subsequent death. There are approximately 40 breeds registered with the American Kennel Club that require tail docking and no breeder of any of these breeds, whether large, such as the Bouvier des Flandres, or small, like the Yorkshire Terrier, takes the docking of tails lightly. No matter how one looks at it, docking is surgery, regardless of how minor it might be, and all surgical precautions must be taken before, during and after the docking process.

BIS winner, Ch. Wil-B's Spicer Hi-Steps, bred and owned by Bernard and Wilma Griffith, Michigan.
K. Booth

Multi-BIS winner, Ch. Pine Hollow's Peter Pan, bred by N. Leon Duffer and W.R. Ptomey, owned by Linda Kazan Stevens and W.L. Aston, Kentucky.
Twomey

14

Ear Cropping

EAR CROPPING, or the surgical removal of a portion of the ear cartilage, has a historical function in many breeds whose ears were cropped to prevent injury, damage and infection. Today, however, ear cropping is mainly done for aesthetic, cosmetic considerations and, in some breeds, as a necessity dictated by the national breed club in its standard of perfection for the breed.

Miniature Pinschers may be shown cropped or uncropped. Many breeders prefer the finished cropped elegance to the so-called plainness of the natural ear and maintain that the stress to the dog, if the cropping is properly done, is minimal. Other breeders do not like the ordeal their dogs must endure in order to have their ears cropped and, if they are sure the ears will be able to stand erect on their own, will not crop them. Some dogs are being cropped because there is fear that the ears will not mature to an erect stance. The lesser the ear to be held up, it is believed, the better the opportunity for it to stay up. A folded-over ear is not permitted in any Miniature Pinscher destined for an American show career as our standard says, "Ears: Set high, standing erect from base to tip."

Cropping is an art and should never be performed by a novice. Only an experienced, specialist cropper or veterinarian familiar with current show styles and fashion should attempt the task on a properly anesthetized dog, who is both physically and mentally healthy. It is necessary to study the dog's head type, ear length and carriage to determine what crop is best suited to the animal. Since dogs are cropped as young puppies, usually 16 or 17 weeks of age, it is essential to project the skull and muzzle as it will appear at maturity and crop accordingly. A short muzzle and broad skull will want an ear that leads the visionary line upward and tapering. A long muzzle might need a longer ear to achieve the appearance of balanced proportions.

The person some breeders have described as the father of present ear trims designed to enhance appearance and elegance is Dr. Buris R. Boshell, of Bo-Mar Kennels in Alabama. He favored the long, sculptured trims that had been adopted for Boxers by a friend of his in Massachusetts. When Dr. Boshell moved to Alabama, he worked with his local veterinarian to copy those trims. In describing his method of ear trimming, or cropping, he says:

> The ears were measured in length usually by pulling the ear over to the medial canthus of the eye and marking the length in this manner. We then used a straight clamp down across the ear and trimmed most of the ear using a safety razor blade. The remaining portion of the trimming was done freehand with a razor blade in order to give a fine tip to the ear and a little curve. We also were very careful to trim off the bell so that one would not end up with a batwing appearance.
>
> Just as important as trimming is the after care of the ear. It is important to keep the cut edge under a mild degree of tension to prevent puckering. Stitches should be taken out within approximately one week's time. Obviously, the minimum number of stitches that can be used to provide adequate support is desirable. We always generally kept an antibiotic ointment on the cut edge of the ear until healing was complete. Furacin, Polysporin and so forth suffice quite well for this. If the ear does not stand after the edge is completely healed, we generally use some thick two-inch tape and make large diamond squares of the tape, about 2 by 2, putting one of the points of the diamond at the tip of the ear and making the ear stand against the taped shape. We leave the ears rolled from four to five days at a time and then take them down again to see how they will stand.

138

One veterinarian who has been successful with proper show trims is Gordon Lawler, DVM, of Anderson, Indiana. He offers this guide for experienced professionals to consider:

The main objective of ear cropping is to provide a neat, alert appearance that conforms to the standard of the breed. An ear crop done improperly (such as too short, too long or too wide) will not present an appearance that is in the right proportion to the size of the head. The mechanics of the surgery will be the same in any breed of dog, with exception to the length of the ear which will be determined by the particular dog and will depend on the width and length of forehead. For example, a dog with a broad head may need longer ears to be in proper proportion to the head, whereas a dog with a narrower head may need a shorter ear for the same reason.

Under general anesthesia, the ears are aseptically prepared for surgery. The first procedure is to determine the length of ear. On most Miniature Pinschers, this will be about three-fourths of the length of the ear. Length is determined by folding the ear back upon itself and marking the fold. The ear is straightened to full length and the tip is brought back to the mark of the previous fold.

After the length is marked on the front edge of the ear, the ear should be drawn forward across the forehead to the inner corner of the opposite eye to see if the mark coincides with the inner corner of the opposite eye. If this mark does not come to the inner corner of the opposite eye, the ear may need to be lengthened some. If it goes beyond this point, it may need to be shortened. This method allows by sight to determine the length of ear to be in proportion to the size of the head considering the length and width of the top of the head.

After length is determined and marked, a cut is made one-eighth inch from the front edge of the ear. A straight intestinal forcep is applied from this point down to and beside the first cartilage protrusion on the inner side of the ear cartilage. A cut is made along the back side of the forceps with the scalpel, removing the rear portion of the ear flap. The forceps are removed and a pair of serrated ear trim scissors are used to continue around the base of the ear opening and around the front edge to remove the cartilage that protrudes at the front edge of the ear canal. This allows the ear to blend into the head when looking at the dog from a front view.

Some people prefer more bell, thinking that the ear will stand better. I have not found this to be an advantage and do not feel that it presents as neat an appearance.

The 1957 style of short ears.
Frank Ashbey is the
handler of Duke of Fremont.
Shafer

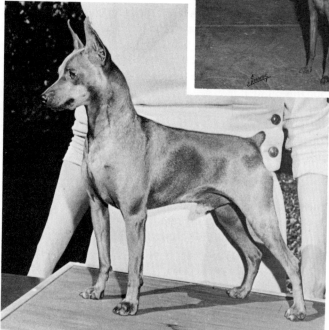

Properly cropped ears will enhance an already
beautiful head. Ch. Bo-Mar's Road Runner,
owned by Mr. and Mrs. William Kleinmanns.

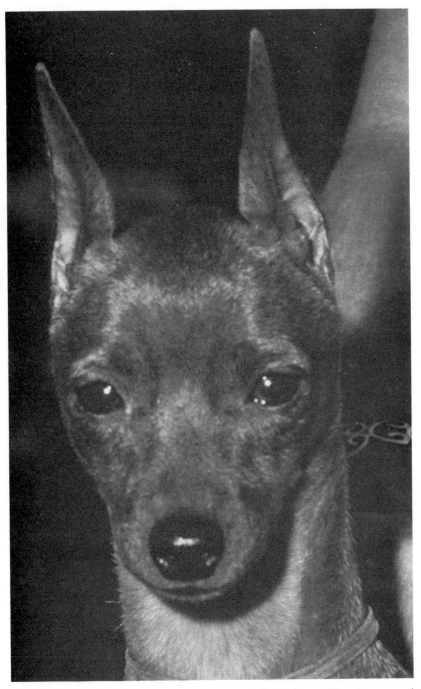

Tall ears designed to bring the viewer's eye upward. Ch. Blythewood I'm a Star, owned and bred by Joan Huber.

The ear is sutured with appropriate suture material starting one-half inch from the tip with either continuous or interrupted sutures down around the base of the ear canal and around the front edge. The sutures should not start at the top of the ear for two reasons: first, if there is excessive tissue reaction from sutures, scar tissue may cause the ears to curl in at the tips; and secondly, suturing all the way to the tip of the ears may cause an undesirable hook in the tip of the ear if there is excessive tissue build-up from the sutures.

At this time, the tip of the ear is taped lightly for three days, at which time the ear seals together and the tape is removed. The sutures are removed in nine days. Should any additional taping be required, it should be done upon suture removal.

It cannot be emphasized strongly enough that cropping is serious surgery to perform on any dog. The puppy must be in good health, past the teething period and stable in mind. Care should be taken at all times that the equipment used is sterilized and the surroundings are clean and quiet. The trimming of the ears should be done only by individuals who are knowledgeable, patient and careful, and who have a good "eye" for the breed's conformation. Each of the 14 different breeds or varieties that may be cropped in the United States call for different styles, based on breed and head type. It is imperative that the cropper be familiar with those styles and trim the ears accordingly. Unfortunate is the experience where an improper crop results in recropping or, in the case of a show dog, becomes a negative factor in adjudicating the animal in the ring. A poor crop can make a head appear to have unsuitable configuration just as a good crop may enhance an otherwise poor head.

As if cropping, or ear trimming, was not enough to think about, the ears have to be carefully attended to once the operation is over. It is necessary to be on guard against possible infection, hence the use of an antibiotic. It is also vital to watch puppies and not let them play in any manner that could lead to harming a newly trimmed ear.

Even after trimming, some Min Pins' ears will not stand up on their own. Many breeders try using supports through wrapping and taping to accomplish this. Frank and Joan Coluccio, Jafco Kennels, New York, Min Pin and Doberman breeders, share their process for taping the ears after cropping and healing:

Make sure edges are healed. If there are any adhesions on edges, the ear has to be pulled and adhesions removed before taping. If you do not know what adhesions are, check with your veterinarian.

Cut tape for each ear as follows: 1 piece 3" long, 3 pieces 1" long, 1 piece 6" long.

Put the dog on a grooming table, facing toward you, and pull the ear straight up, holding it stiff. Take the 3" piece of tape and apply lengthwise up the outer edge of the ear. Take 2 pieces of the 1" tape and place them diagonally over the lengthwise tape in two different spots in the middle of the ear where it would probably fold when not taped if unable to stand on its own. The third piece should be placed on a slight diagonal line up and down similar to the first piece.

Take the 6" piece of tape and affix it to the base of the ear on the tape that is already applied. Stretch the ear, folding the edges inward, and starting at the base begin winding this 6" strip around the ear, rolling the ear inward at the same time as taping. Continue this to the tip of the ear.

Repeat this process with the other ear.

Cut another piece of tape, length depending on width of topskull and ears. Starting at the base of one of the ears, roll the tape around that ear and reach to the other ear going around that base as well. Reinforce this bridge tape with another piece of tape for security.

Ears should be checked every day to make sure that there is no odor. If there is odor, remove tape at once and look for an infection. Do not attempt to retape until infection is totally cleared. If there is no odor, leave tape on for at least five to seven days and then remove with nail polish remover.

If after removing tape, ears do not stand and are not sore, massage them where the ear is bending by moving your thumb and forefinger together on the bend. Do this for a period of ten minutes four or five times a day and retape within 24 hours.

If the ears are sore, clean with alcohol or peroxide, and use vitamin E or Desitin on the sore spots. Always clean again with alcohol after the ear is healed and before you start to tape again.

Keep up this procedure until the ears stand. They may possibly stand for a few days and then fall. If this happens, start immediately with the retaping procedure as above. Do not leave down and *do not give up*.

Cleanliness is important with the entire procedure.

15

The Natural Ear

THE NUMBER OF MINIATURE PINSCHER breeders in America who prefer the "natural," i.e., uncropped or untrimmed, ear is increasing and more dogs' ears are being left in their natural state. Countries abroad, such as England and Germany, and down under, like Australia, forbid the cropping of ears. There is a firm belief by several American breeders that this country may some day follow suit. Already several states ban cropping and the humane societies are becoming more vocal on the subject of classifying cropping as inhumane.

Breeders who oppose cropping do so because of the stress and discomfort it causes the dogs, potential for shock, high cost and inability to find enough experienced persons who are capable of properly cropping ears. An opinion has long been expressed that cropping serves no purpose other than man's desire to manufacture a dog's appearance.

In Germany, cropping only became illegal effective January 1, 1987. The current breed standard states:

> Up until January 1, 1987, when ear cropping became legally disallowed in Germany, the ears were usually cropped; however, ear cropping was not a requirement. No dogs whelped in Germany after January 1, 1987 may be registered and/or shown in shows sponsored by the Verband fuer das Deutsche Hundewesen (German Association for Dog Breeding) with cropped ears.

In Australia, folded or dropped ears are permitted.

Some young American puppies have folded ears until time of cropping and taping.

Dogs whelped before January 1, 1987: Dogs with cropped ears must have uniformly cropped ears, set high and held erectly.

Uncropped ears: ears must be set high, V-shaped with a fold; or ears must be small and erect, whereby both ears must be held uniformly erect.

Mike Towell, of Zwergpin Kennels in Australia, says of his country:

We are not allowed to crop ears in Australia. However, at present there is no restriction on the docking of tails or the removal of dewclaws. If we import a cropped ear animal, we are forbidden, by Kennel Club Regulations, to exhibit these animals in competition.

In England, ear cropping was abolished by the Kennel Club on July 1, 1903. Fred Leonard, of Lionlike Min Pins in England, describes the present status:

You can have cropped dogs in this country, and the ones seen here come from the Continent and America. However, you would not be able to find a vet in this country to do the job. The reason no one bothers to crop is because no cropped dog is allowed to compete or "be present at" a show run under Kennel Club rules. A friend of mine has a German import Min Pin who is cropped but the Kennel Club refused permission for him to go to any shows. We are now part of the Common Market and there are moves afoot in Brussels to ban "cropping and docking."

Unlike the American standard which is specific in only permitting "erect" ears, the English Miniature Pinscher standard says, "Ears: Must be set high, as small as possible, erect or dropped." The dropped ear is referred to as a tightly folded terrier-type ear. In Germany, high-set ears, V-shaped, with a fold are permitted. Several American breeders privately admit that they would not crop ears if the American standard would follow the footsteps of these countries and others and allow ears that fold over to be eligible for dog shows.

Many of the American breeders who are advocating and showing natural eared dogs maintain that their animals are not getting the same consideration in the show ring as their cropped

In Germany, small, erect, uncropped ears are required in the breed standard.

Two natural eared American Min Pins owned by Lerae Britain, Hawaii. Behind the dogs is a beautiful stained glass art piece crafted by Ms. Britain.

Zandor Hey Pepsi is another natural eared Min Pin owned by Lerae Britain. The dog is one-half Australian, one-half U.S. breeding.

Another American breeder who advocates the natural look is Shawn Brown. This black and rust female is Baroness Gillian von Hatten.

brothers. While it may take judges time to get used to the different appearance of a natural ear, a good quality dog, regardless of its ear, will always shine. There are some individuals who believe that all that is needed for the natural look to catch on is to have someone extensively campaign and promote a superior dog with small, erect natural ears.

Candids by Connie

Every puppy deserves a loving home and conscientious breeders go out of their way to assure that the prospective buyers are able to provide for the puppy.

Candids by Connie

16

Puppies, Breeders and Clubs

TRYING TO UNITE THE "RIGHT" PUPPY with the "right" buyer is always a prime consideration for every serious breeder, regardless of his breed. A Min Pin breeder is no different, as he or she knows that this active, little toy dog will make a wonderful pet and companion for someone who is eager and willing to devote the time, care and attention that the animal deserves. Similarly, any prospective buyer wants to purchase a healthy, happy pup with whom to share a lifetime.

Every breeder should ask a prospective buyer a myriad of questions concerning a potential buyer's background, dog knowledge, desires and intentions. Conversely, a prospective buyer should be able to personally visit with the puppy that is for sale, see its dam, litter mates, if any, and discuss with the breeder the pup's health, shots and general care. It is expected that both the buyer and seller would be wary of each other. They have a lot at stake, but it is the puppy, itself, who has the most to lose if it is purchased by a buyer who is ill-equipped to care for him.

No one should ever buy a Min Pin if they are not prepared to devote time, effort and money to the dog's well-being. Not only must the dog's health be carefully looked after and periodic shots and checkups attended to, but every degree of the dog's life will demand mindful attention. Is the animal being fed good dog food? Is his vitamin intake adequate? Is he properly bathed? Are his home surroundings clean and pleasant? Does he have toys to play with? A comfortable bed? And, perhaps most important of all, are his human relationships fun, loving and plentiful? If a potential owner is not willing to dedicate a lot of time and a fair amount of expense to overseeing the well-being, comfort and companionship of a dog, then he should not consider such a purchase in the first place.

Anyone who is interested in buying a Miniature Pinscher, or wants to learn more about the breed, should attend local dog shows and talk with breeders. The American Kennel Club, 51 Madison Avenue, New York, New York 10010 has a list of all-breed and specialty clubs that lie within a specific area. A letter or telephone call can secure the names and addresses of the organizations' secretaries, who in turn can be called for breed and show information.

With this data, a prospective Min Pin buyer should attend shows and communicate with breeders by telephone or letters expressing interest in the breed. Kennels should never be visited without first calling for an appointment. No kennel owner appreciates or is likely to help someone who fails to exhibit common good manners.

Many Min Pin breeders will wait and not sell their pups until after the ears are cropped and healed. Others, however, who do not have ears trimmed let puppies go to new homes as soon as they are stable, beyond initial shots and functioning independently.

It is good for new owners of Min Pins to maintain contact with the breeder who sold them the puppy. If there are any questions, doubts or problems, they should not hesitate to turn to the breeder for advice. Newcomers to the breed who want to learn more about the breed could profit from belonging to the national parent breed club, regional breed club or both. The Miniature Pinscher breed is fortunate in having an active national breed parent club, the Miniature Pinscher Club of America, which works diligently to promote and protect the breed. The club has a national publication,

The Pinscher Patter, and serves as an excellent reference for assistance, guidance and local breeder information.

In addition to the national breed parent club, MPCA, there are twelve regional breed clubs. Five of these clubs are AKC approved specialty clubs who can sponsor regional specialty shows, while the remaining seven are working toward that status. Regional clubs presently holding specialty events are:

> Empire Miniature Pinscher Club
> > New York, New York area
> > Presently sponsors one independent specialty a year, usually in February
> Yankee Miniature Pinscher Club
> > Springfield, Massachusetts/New England area
> > Presently holds May and November specialty shows
> Dallas Miniature Pinscher Club
> > Dallas, Texas area
> > Specialties scheduled in March and September
> Miniature Pinscher Club of Greater Tucson
> > Tucson, Arizona area
> > November specialty show
> Miniature Pinscher Club of Greater Los Angeles
> > Southern California area
> > Newly approved for specialty show status

Regional clubs that do not provide specialty shows at this time:

> Tarheel Miniature Pinscher Club
> > North and South Carolina area
> Miniature Pinscher Club of the Deep South
> > Louisiana, Mississippi and Alabama area
> Midwest Miniature Pinscher Club
> > Chicago area
> Texoma Miniature Pinscher Club
> > Ft. Worth, Texas area
> Miniature Pinscher Club of Houston
> > Houston, Texas area

153

Miniature Pinscher Club of Greater Phoenix
Phoenix, Arizona area
Pacific Northwest Miniature Pinscher Club
Portland, Oregon and Seattle, Washington area

One of the main purposes of a breed club is to sponsor special exhibitions devoted entirely to the breed. These events, which are called specialty shows, may be held in conjunction with an all-breed show or by themselves as independents. The first independent national specialty show sponsored by the Miniature Pinscher Club of America was held in Chicago, April 4, 1964. Prior to that time, all specialties were held in conjunction with an all-breed event. In the fall of 1972 the parent club elected to hold two national specialties per year. The first is called the Spring National and the second called the Fall National, each being of equal importance. However, starting in the spring of 1987 the national club chose to revert to the old system of putting all effort into one independent specialty. This event is held in the spring of every year and moves around the country according to the membership desires.

MCPA National Independent Specialty Winners, as compiled by David M. Krogh, club president 1986 and 1987, are:

4/4/64	Chicago, IL	Judge: Heywood Hartley
	BOB:	Ch. Shieldcrest Cinnamon Toast (D)
	Owner:	Mrs. Boyce Bailes
	Breeder:	Clare C. Curtin
4/2/65	Chicago, IL	Judge: E.W. Tipton, Jr.
	BOB:	Ch. Bo-Mar's Drummer Boy (D)
	Owner:	Dr. Buris Boshell
	Breeder:	Owner
4/1/66	Chicago, IL	Judge: Louis Murr
	BOB:	Ch. Rebel Roc's Jackpot (D)
	Owner:	Mrs. Madeline Condon
	Breeder:	Mrs. E.W. Tipton, Jr.
7/21/67	Chicago, IL	Judge: Percy Roberts
	BOB:	Ch. Rebel Roc's Star Boarder (D)
	Owner:	Dr. Buris Boshell
	Breeder:	Mrs. E.W. Tipton, Jr.

4/5/68	Chicago, IL	Judge: Phil Marsh

BOB: Ch. Rebel Roc's Star Boarder (D)
Owner: Dr. Buris Boshell
Breeder: Mrs. E.W. Tipton, Jr.

4/4/69 Chicago, IL Judge: Mrs. Van Court

BOB: Ch. Helms Nero (D)
Owner: Bill and Sue Allen
Breeder: Maynard W. and Joyce Helms

4/3/70 Chicago, IL Judge: Alva Rosenberg
BOB: Ch. Jay-Mac's Jacqueline (B)
Owner: Mr. and Mrs. John McNamara
Breeder: Mrs. Madeline Condon

4/2/71 Chicago, IL Judge: Langdon Skarda
BOB: Ch. Allens Brandy Snifter (D)
Owner: Bill and Sue Allen
Breeder: Owners

3/31/72 Chicago, IL Judge: Robert Waters
BOB: Star-M Trace of Scarlet (B)
Owner: Don and Shirley Meyers
Breeder: Owners

9/22/72 Dallas, TX Judge: Joe Gregory
BOB: Jay-Mac's Candy Man (D)
Owner: Mr. and Mrs. John McNamara
Breeder: Owners

3/30/73 Chicago, IL Judge: E.W. Tipton, Jr.
BOB: Ch. Jay-Mac's Impossible Dream (B)
Owner: Dorothy H. Turco
Breeder: Mr. and Mrs. John McNamara

10/5/73 Portland, OR Judge: Robert C. Hatch, Jr.
BOB: Ch. K-Roc's Black Doubloon (D)
Owner: David and Sharon Krogh
Breeder: Owner

3/29/74 Chicago, IL Judge: Harold Bishop
BOB: Ch. Jay-Mac's Pat Hand (D)
Owner: Jack Phelan and John McNamara
Breeder: Mr. and Mrs. John McNamara

155

Min Pins are happy with children who are taught how to treat them with respect and love.

Mickey Carmichael is shown working on her famed Ch. Sir Ius of the Hill trophy, assisted by her Min Pin friends. This porcelain statuette was originally presented for BOB at the Miniature Pinscher Club of America Specialty in Houston and was won by Ch. Patzie von Mill-Mass.

9/20/74   Dallas, TX   Judge: Edd E. Bivin
                 BOB: Ch. Jay-Mac's Impossible Dream (B)
                 Owner: Dorothy DeMaria
                 Breeder: Mr. and Mrs. John McNamara
3/28/75   Chicago, IL   Judge: Maxine Beam
                 BOB: Ch. Top Hat Arabella (B)
                 Owner: Juanette Woodie and
                               Jeanne Crutchfield
                 Breeder: Neal Tadlock and A. Schomber
9/19/75   Dallas, TX   Judge: Peter Knoop
                 BOB: Ch. Jay-Mac's Impossible Dream (B)
                 Owner: Dorothy DeMaria
                 Breeder: Mr. and Mrs. John McNamara
3/26/76   Chicago, IL   Judge: Joe Gregory
                 BOB: Ch. Jay-Mac's Dream Walking (B)
                 Owner: Jack Phelan and John McNamara
                 Breeder: Mr. and Mrs. John McNamara
10/22/76   Tempe, AZ   Judge: Michele Billings
                 BOB: Mercer's Desert Dust Devil (D)
                 Owner: Irene Kloeber and Frank Mercer, Jr.
                 Breeder: Kay Bergeron
4/1/77   Chicago, IL   Judge: Glen M. Sommers
                 BOB: Reh-Mont's I Got Rhythm (D)
                 Owner: Mr. and Mrs. Harmon Montgomery
                 Breeder: Owners
11/25/77   Springfield, MA   Judge: Michele Billings
                 BOB: Ch. Mercer's Desert Dust Devil (D)
                 Owner: Irene Kloeber
                 Breeder: Kay Bergeron
3/31/78   Chicago, IL   Judge: Robert Waters
                 BOB: Ch. Mercer's Desert Dust Devil (D)
                 Owner: Irene Kloeber
                 Breeder: Kay Bergeron
10/6/78   Pasadena, CA   Judge: Joe Gregory
                 BOB: Ch. Joy's Lady Ginger (B)
                 Owner: Al and Dee Stutts
                 Breeder: John and Helen Yarwood   157

3/30/79	Chicago, IL	Judge:	Phil Marsh
	BOB:	Ch. Shinyas Pipe Dream (B)	
	Owner:	Sue Neville	
	Breeder:	Owner	

9/21/79	Mexquite, TX	Judge:	Dorothy Nickles
	BOB:	Ch. Pine Hollow's Peter Pan (D)	
	Owner:	Linda Kazan and W.L. Aston	
	Breeder:	Leon Duffer and W.R. Ptomey, MD	

3/28/80	Chicago, IL	Judge:	Frank Nishimura
	BOB:	Ch. Mercer's Desert Dust Devil (D)	
	Owner:	Irene Kloeber	
	Breeder:	Kay Bergeron	

11/21/80	Springfield, MA	Judge:	Norm Patton
	BOB:	Ch. Onlyone Bon Bon (B)	
	Owner:	Tom Baldwin and B. Bushey	
	Breeder:	Tom Baldwin	

3/27/81	Chicago, IL	Judge:	Toshikazu Uryu
	BOB:	Ch. Fillpin's Serendipity (B)	
	Owner:	Dave and Judy Fillpot	
	Breeder:	Owners	

9/18/81	Irving, TX	Judge:	Derek Rayne
	BOB:	Ch. Shajawn Semi Tough (D)	
	Owner:	Dorothy Hazel and Betty Moore	
	Breeder:	Linda Talbot	

4/2/82	Chicago, IL	Judge:	Michele Billings
	BOB:	Ch. Carlee Nubby Silk (D)	
	Owner:	Marcia Tucker	
	Breeder:	Ann Dutton and Carol Garrison	

7/30/82	Santa Barbara, CA	Judge:	Del Glodowski
	BOB:	Ch. Carlee Nubby Silk (D)	
	Owner:	Marcia Tucker	
	Breeder:	Ann Dutton and Carol Garrison	

4/1/83	Chicago, IL	Judge:	David Krogh
	BOB:	Ch. Mercer's Desert Dust Devil (D)	
	Owner:	Irene Kloeber	
	Breeder:	Kay Bergeron	

Specialties sponsored by the breed clubs are wonderful venues for sharing experiences, learning and enjoying companionship with other dog lovers. Judy Fillpot handles her homebred, Ch. Fillpin's Serendipity, to BOB in 1981. Trophy presenter in the middle is John McNamara, while the gentleman to the right is Ralph Lemcke. The judge is Toshikazu Uryu from Japan.   *Ritter*

Linda Kazan Stevens brings her pride, Ch. Pine Hollow's Peter Pan, out of retirement to win the 1986 specialty from the Veterans Class. The judge was E.W. Tipton, Jr.

K. Booth

A Galaxy of American Show Dogs

National specialty winner Ch. Bee Jay's Photo Finish, bred and owned by Bob and Billie Jean Shuler, Washington. *Lindemaier*

BIS winner Ch. Shajawn Semi Tough, owned by Dorothy M. Hazel and Betty Moore, bred by Linda Talbot, Texas. *Pegin*

Ch. Baron von Luchenback, bred and owned by Dorothy M. Hazel and Betty Moore, Texas. *Missy*

Multi-group winner Ch. Carovel's Jasmine, bred and owned by Caroline Ofenloch, Pennsylvania. *Ashbey*

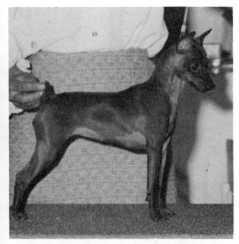

Ch. Ric-Lor's Toyota, owned by Caroline Ofenloch and bred by Claire L. Panichi, Pennsylvania.

Cain

BIS winner Ch. Wil-B's Sundance Kid, bred and owned by Bernard and Wilma Griffith, Michigan.

Graham

Ch. Alster-Elbe Red Firecracker, bred and owned by Hildegard Olin, Minnesota.

Ch. Halrok Hot Ticket, bred and owned by Vera Halpin Bistrim, New York City.

Shafer

11/18/83   Tucson, AZ   Judge: Thomas Conway
BOB: Ch. Carlee Nubby Silk (D)
Owner: Marcia Tucker
Breeder: Ann Dutton and Carol Garrison

6/8/84   Tampa, FL   Judge: Kenneth Miller
BOB: Ch. Sanbrook Simplicity (B)
Owner: Nancy Gwynne
Breeder: Ann Dutton

11/16/84   Philadelphia, PA   Judge: Sari B. Tietjen
BOB: Ch. Sanbrook Sahara (B)
Owner: Ann Walker
Breeder: Ann Dutton

1/18/85   Vancouver, WA   Judge: Robert Waters
BOB: Ch. Mercer's Desert Dust Devil (D)
Owner: Irene Kloeber
Breeder: Kay Bergeron

9/18/85   Irving, TX   Judge: Charles Bordelon
BOB: Ch. Sunsprite Saxon of Carlee (D)
Owner: Tom Baldwin and Marcia Tucker
Breeder: Carol Garrison and Marcia Tucker

3/14/86   Louisville, KY   Judge: E.W. Tipton, Jr.
BOB: Ch. Pine Hollow's Peter Pan (D)
Owner: Linda Kazan
Breeder: Leon Duffer and W.R. Ptomey, MD

10/4/86   Anaheim, CA   Judge: Sharon A. Krogh
BOB: Ch. Bee Jay's Photo Finish (D)
Owner: Bob and Billie Jean Shuler
Breeder: Billie Jean Shuler

5/7/87   West Springfield, MA   Judge: Betty Moore
BOB: Ch. Pevensey's Cash Dividend (D)
Owner: Pam Ruggie and Marcia Tucker
Breeder: Pam Ruggie

17

Health Care

MINIATURE PINSCHERS ARE hardy dogs. They usually have good appetites, a lot of energy and simple requirements. They are active companions who require little care. As with all dogs, however, there is a need to keep up with inoculations, vitamins and quality dog food. Some breeders supplement their dogs by giving them vitamin E for their skin and calcium for their bones.

Demodectic mange, fairly common in several smooth-coated breeds, is also seen in Min Pins. In order to prevent this one breeder gives her dogs 100 I.U. of vitamin E daily, together with spraying the animals with a mixture of Alpha Keri Bath Oil and water (20 parts water to one part oil). Another uses Goodwinol Oil, while Ben and Vickie Jones, of Ben-Lyn Kennels in West Virginia, have found Fungisan (manufactured by Tomlyn) to be excellent in healing and promoting the quick return of hair growth.

Sometimes dogs will experience an allergic reaction to the antigens present in immunization and booster shots. One breeder's veterinarian prescribed Chlor-Timetron Syrup (an over-the-counter antihistamine) to be given orally at one teaspoon per dose on this schedule:

> 1st dose—evening prior to injection
> 2nd dose—morning of injection

3rd dose—evening of injection
4th dose—morning of day after injection
5th dose—evening of day after injection

Proper care of the teeth is a must. John McNamara, of the famed Jay-Mac Min Pins, offers some thoughts and suggestions:

The Miniature Pinscher, being a small breed with a small chiseled head and muzzle, has little room for mistakes or carelessness in their teething and care of their teeth, especially when getting the second set, or permanent teeth.

Many toy breeds do not shed baby teeth easily or on their own initiative. Many tooth-related problems, such as missing teeth, overshot or undershot bite, are caused by not getting the milk or baby teeth out of the way so the permanent teeth can come in straight or unopposed by the non-shed baby teeth. I have seen some good young Min Pins with almost two complete sets of teeth, neither one in the right position.

When I first started breeding Min Pins, some of my dogs had teeth problems and I worked a system to eliminate them. I keep a close eye on the young puppy from four months of age upward to watch for when the gums start to swell and the front baby teeth start to loosen a bit. When this happens, I have the four front baby upper incisors removed at the same time. I do not remove the lower incisors until the four uppers are fairly well established, but as the lower front teeth begin to appear, I remove the baby teeth that are in the way. By doing this, I get the front of the bite pretty well established with the four upper and lower teeth in the same line. The next teeth I look after are the lower canine, or eye teeth. If they are not gotten out of the way, the permanent canines can come in on the inside and interfere with the roof of the puppy's mouth. The upper canines can stay a bit longer, but should be removed as soon as the permanent canines appear. I have experienced little trouble with the teeth in back of the canines, but of course those teeth must also be taken out as the permanent molars appear.

Unless you are very experienced and know what you are doing, a veterinarian is the best person to take care of the teeth. It is quite easy to break a small jaw bone, or cause a young puppy to fear mouth inspection because of poor handling during teething.

All dogs' teeth, especially show dogs, should be kept clean. This can be done with a small toothbrush or rough towel, using a paste made of a little salt or soda and water.

Even "Little Daddy" liked to play.

An older Min Pin—loved, comforted, and properly looked after—will live many years, giving his owners a lot of love and joy in return.

165

Some breeders also use hydrogen peroxide applied with a cotton swab for weekly teeth cleaning. If one is gentle and makes a game out of the exercise, the dog will not object and the end result will be healthy gums and clean, white teeth.

As with all dogs, it is necessary to keep the Min Pin clean. If the dog begins to smell "like a dog," then he should be bathed in a gentle detergent and towel dried with a cotton terry. Ears should be checked for wax buildup and toenails examined to see if shortening is needed.

Since Min Pins are known for being both inquisitive and active, owners are always looking out for situations where their dog might hurt itself. Potentially poisonous products are kept out of the way. Efforts are made to keep jumping on and off furniture at a minimum. A broken leg may be the result of a poor jump and good veterinary care is a must in order to assure proper healing.

Older Min Pins are not as active as they had been in their younger years, when they were sprightly and curious and getting into everything around them. A breeder offers this advice for owners with older dogs:

> I think the most important thing to do is give them a comfortable place to sleep and an area that they can call their own. Older dogs tend to wear off hair, get callouses on the elbows and so forth, so providing them with a good, soft, clean bed and occasionally bathing them and putting oil on their elbows, hips and so forth is very much indicated. One should refrain from getting the dog too fat and should allow him to have regular exercise.

Since cataracts are known to develop in some Min Pins as they age, several breeders recommend using Catacollirium, or zinc ascorbate drops, under veterinarian supervision, in an effort to treat this condition.

All Miniature Pinscher owners know that they must be careful to avoid situations where the animals might harm themselves. As Min Pins are active, both in mind and body, this can be a full-time, albeit never dull, task! Indeed, the inquisitive nature that often gets the little dogs into trouble is one of their most endearing traits. They are a challenge to own and a delight to love.

166

18

Training

SINCE THE MINIATURE PINSCHER is a willful, determined little dog, always trying to outfox its master, training should never be left until last. Puppies need to be worked with as soon as they are old enough to be aware of their surroundings. It is important that they be picked up, cuddled and talked to from very early on so that they come to regard human beings as friends and a source of comfort and love. They should be frequently played with and toys for them to chew need to be kept readily at hand.

All Min Pins, regardless of whether they are destined to be show dogs or pets, should be leash broken and table trained. Nancy and Kent Grusendorf, Von Dorf Kennels, follow this schedule:

Socialization

21 days old	Keep puppies near most active area. Handle and cuddle pups.
3–4 weeks	Even though pups are getting more active, they must be kept with their dam to ensure sound temperament development.
4 weeks	Give pups every possible human contact. Get down with them, touch and talk, at least ten minutes twice daily.
6 weeks	Give individual attention.

Puppies need training at an early age, including how to properly stand on a table.
Candids by Connie

And when the puppy grows up, he will also be able to free stand while on the ground. Amy Putnam stands holding Ch. Ampins Lit'l Rascal O' Larcon on a loose lead in a show poise. Sari Tietjen is the judge.
Missy

168

Training

6 weeks	Place a soft collar around the pup's neck for five minutes daily.
7 weeks	Snap a lightweight lead to the collar and let it drag on the floor or ground while the pup walks around for five minutes daily.
8–10 weeks	Stress period. Avoid fear-producing experiences.
11 weeks	Begin table training:

    1. Be slow, gentle and reassuring.

    2. Lower pup's rear onto table first.

    3. Stretch pup's body to full length and then lower front.

    4. Hold for pup's security and reaction.

    5. If calm, remove hands one at a time. If pup refuses to stand, hold gently yet firmly in position saying, "Easy, stay, good puppy."

    6. Stand for two minutes twice daily on table.

Begin lead training:

    1. Lead train by reassuring and following puppy on its first outing. The second and subsequent outings, encourage puppy to follow (using toys or food as an enticement, if necessary). Let pup move ahead of you if he takes the lead and if you can maintain control.

    2. Lead train with short playful sessions, gradually increasing one minute every other day to no more than two half-hour sessions daily at five months of age. Once lead trained, discontinue training immediately— don't overdo or you may lose pup's natural showmanship. Always include a play session at end of each training session.

5½ months	Stop pup to stand and pose. After tight lead, slack off and work loose. Take to shopping

169

centers for exposure to sights, sounds and people. Use common sense and much reassurance.

Dr. Buris R. Boshell, Bo-Mar Kennels, offers his thoughts on the subject:

> As the puppies grow and develop I think it is important they be socialized, taught to stand on the table and be taught to beg for tidbits in order to make good showmen.
>
> It is a good idea to let visitors that come to the home handle the puppies on the table so that they do not shy away from strangers. Frequently it is helpful to take the puppies on a lead, as soon as you get them reasonably well lead broken, into a shopping center where they are really around crowds.
>
> I find the best way to lead break is to take a trained dog out with the green puppy, having placed a soft collar and / or lead around the puppy's neck. Using cheese, vienna sausages or raw hamburger as bait, I have the old dog and the puppy follow me around. As soon as the puppy is no longer concerned about dragging the leash around, I will usually take hold of the leash and slowly let the puppy know that I am guiding him. All the time, of course, I am enticing him with tidbits.
>
> The training session should be no more than five to fifteen minutes at a time, and one should have a puppy quite well lead trained within no more than four or five days.

Training the Min Pin for the conformation show ring should be relatively easy if the above suggestions are followed. A Min Pin that has been properly raised and acquainted with society is a natural showman. He needs little "hands-on" attention as he will strut out at the end of the lead while gaiting and stand pert and alert, with four feet solidly beneath him, when still. Unlike other breeds, this hands-off showman requires little assistance from the person on the other end of the lead. All he really needs is a little guidance and control.

There has been a recent trend among newer exhibitors and handlers, however, to attempt to stack their dogs instead of letting them show themselves off naturally. Old-timers deplore this tendency to artificially show the breed since its naturalness is one of its unique features. John McNamara, Jay-Mac, offers these comments on the subject:

170

There is entirely too much stacking of Miniature Pinschers on the show floor—in some cases, so much pawing, moving and handling that the dogs become upset and ruin their chances. I've heard judges tell some handlers, "Leave the dog alone and let him show himself."

A few years back it was a no-no to stack a Min Pin on the floor. A Min Pin was to be shown like a terrier, enabling him to show his animation and spirit on a loose lead as much as possible. When an exhibitor or handler gets down and flounders on the floor, he's usually blocking the judge's view of the dog's good silhouette. The dog should be held out at arm's length so the judge can get a clear, unobstructed view of the animal.

When an exhibitor or handler drops down to prop up the tail or set all four feet, he could be telling the judge where the dog needs help and the judge may agree and select a dog that does well on his own.

I trained my dogs to stand out ahead of me, look at the activity going on around them and pose solid.

No one knows how difficult—or easy—it is to show and live with a Miniature Pinscher than professional handler Joe Waterman of Temple City, California. Joe was the handler of Ch. Jay-Mac's Impossible Dream, owned by Dorothy DeMaria. "Impy," as Impossible Dream is known, was both a delight and challenge for Joe to show. She still holds the breed record of 79 Bests in Show and 175 Group 1sts. Joe recalls a few of his experiences:

I think that every handler should try to show a Min Pin at least once in their career. The little demons can make a fool out of the best of handlers, making them look like a total novice in the ring.

Training the Min Pin for the show ring is one of the most futile undertakings a person can attempt. The Min Pin is very much like a hyperkinetic child. Their attention span is very short. I find it much easier to get their attention if I keep them a little hungry when in the ring and keep flashing pieces of well-seasoned, garlic-flavored liver in front of their noses.

We will sometimes let the young puppies run around the house with a show lead around their neck. The leash part is gathered up and tied with a rubber band. This lets the dog get used to having the lead in place around the neck before any pressure is applied. Again, the liver is flashed in front of their nose while we walk backwards and keep calling the pup by name.

I have found that most Min Pins will not respond to a stranger or

171

Best in Show winner Ch. Fillpin's Red Raider stood perfectly free in a field while his owner/handler, Paulann Phelan, took this picture.

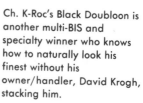

Min Pins, being active and inquisitive, will not always stand with all four feet on the ground. BIS winner Ch. Jothona's Steppin Sabrina, owned by Gerona E. MacCuaig of Canada, would rather play.

Ch. K-Roc's Black Doubloon is another multi-BIS and specialty winner who knows how to naturally look his finest without his owner/handler, David Krogh, stacking him.

Handler Buddy Stevens knows that a pretty young Min Pin bitch is perfectly capable of standing by herself at the end of the lead.

Min Pins sometimes need something to keep their attention from wandering. Bob Condon offers liver to top-winning Ch. Jay-Mac's Dream Walking during a free moment in the ring.

Booth

judge unless they have confidence in their handler. It is sometimes necessary for the handler to have the dog live in the house with them to gain this confidence.

I have found that some bitches, when in season, will go down in the pastern and look flat-footed when put on the table. Also, the feet in both sexes will splay out a little when put on a table that has grooves in the top running the same direction as the dog's body.

Min Pins are great watchdogs. With their keen sense of hearing and loud bark, they sound bigger than they are. They are the King of Toys: fast-footed, very affectionate and protective of their owners.

They don't like the cold too well and will roach their back while on the table or floor if bothered by a draft.

When we first started showing Ch. Jay-Mac's Impossible Dream, she was very leery of noises and occasionally would freak out in the ring. We overcame this situation by constantly walking her next to metal garbage cans and banging the cans until the noise no longer bothered her.

In 1974, I was showing a Bichon for Dorothy Turco of Florida. She also owned "Impy," who was being shown by Dick Vaughn. Dick had already made Impy a multi-group and BIS winner. Mrs. Turco's husband became seriously ill and she called me to ask if I knew anyone who might be interested in buying Impy and continuing her career. We convinced a client, Dorothy "Smokey" DeMaria, to purchase Impy and to retire the Silky Terrier, Brussels Griffon and Miniature Dachshund I was then showing for her.

At that time, I was serving on the Board of the Professional Handlers' Association of America and made plans to pick Impy up from Mrs. Turco in Florida on my way to New York for a board meeting. After the meeting, I boarded the plane for California with Impy in a cat carrier that had a wire mesh top. Impy had totally buried herself under the blanket in the cage. As the plane was backing away from the terminal, the stewardess asked what was in the cage. I told her it was a boa constrictor. She screamed, "No snakes are allowed on the plane in the cabin." She ran forward to get the head stewardess, who also informed me that no snakes were allowed in the cabin. I told her that I had paid excess baggage for the crate and the proper authorities had approved the snake's passage. She then asked to see the snake. I made hissing noises and Impy stuck her nose out from beneath the covers. Both girls screamed. The head stewardess was beside herself since the aircraft was already taxiing down the runway. She walked away and left me alone. When the plane landed in

"Impy," Ch. Jay-Mac's Impossible Dream, was handler Joe Waterman's delight and a beloved show dog who did a lot for the breed. She was top toy in 1975 and 1976.

California and I got ready to get off, Impy stuck her whole head out of the covers and I showed her to the crew.

Impy won the Toy Group at Westminster in 1975. She was Top Toy Dog in 1975 and 1976, winning the Quaker Oats Award for most group wins for a toy those two years. She won 79 BIS and 175 Group 1sts.

She was left to me in the will of the late Dorothy DeMaria and is very active today at the age of 17. She had two single pup litters, both of whom live with us.

19

"Little Daddy"

"**I**MPY" WAS A WONDERFUL SHOW DOG who did much to promote the breed. When she stepped in the ring, everyone watched. There is another dog—a male—who paved the way for Impy and other Miniature Pinschers who later became successful in the show ring. This dog, who stands out in the hearts and minds of serious breeders and exhibitors everywhere, was Ch. Rebel Roc's Casanova von Kurt. "Little Daddy" received a lot of attention wherever his owner, E.W. Tipton, Jr., showed him. It mattered not if the event was large or small, when Little Daddy was present so too was a loyal band of followers. People who had not been previously attracted to toy dogs would not fail to marvel and enjoy this little animal who considered himself to be the king of the dog world. His ringside antics and whirlwind activity bewitched his judges, competitors and spectators alike.

E.W. Tipton, Jr. was a soft-spoken man who always called Tennessee his home. Little Daddy was neither his first show dog nor his first Min Pin, but he was the animal who remained in his heart forever. Tears would come to his eyes when he recalled the wonderful times they had together.

Little Daddy was a joy and challenge to his breeder/owners. Tipton, who had formerly been a sporting dog man, became involved in Min Pins because his wife at that time was attracted to the breed. The first Miniature Pinscher the Tiptons purchased was a five-month-old female puppy from Maisie Booher's Bel-Roc Kennels in West Virginia. This bitch, who quickly finished her championship when she matured, was Ch. Bel-Roc's Sugar von Enztal and she became Little Daddy's granddam. During her show career, Sugar won the national specialty, a Best in Show and ten Group 1sts. She retired to have puppies and was bred to another Best in Show winning Min Pin, Ch. Mudhen Acres Red Snapper, owned by Mr. and Mrs. Hank Hearn of Memphis, Tennessee. This mating resulted in two puppies: one a red male, whom the Tiptons gave away, and the other a black-and-tan female that was described as being "right at the top of the standard." With the advice of Mrs. Booher, Tipton bred this black-and-tan bitch, Rolling Greens Sparkle, to a male he was able to purchase, Ch. Baron Anthony von Mayer. Tip had often stated that Tony, as the dog was called, had an ugly head with a lot of positive features and combined with Sparkle the two complemented each other to produce good progeny. Two particularly well-known offspring of breedings between Sparkle and Tony were a male that came from the first mating, Ch. Rebel Roc's Vanguard von Kurt, and Little Daddy, who came from the second and was whelped September 11, 1958.

Little Daddy was an odd pet name for a dog. Tipton said he named him after one of the characters in *Cat on a Hot Tin Roof.* There were three males in this second mating of Sparkle and Tony. The largest was called Big Daddy, the middle one Middle Daddy and the smallest Little Daddy.

Little Daddy was difficult to leash break and Tip thought he'd never get the dog to show. "He was so wild. I'd turn him flips in the air and he'd come down wagging his tail," Tip was fond of saying. He finally put a choke collar on the little dog and that made the difference that counted. "I think probably at that time I had never seen a Min Pin shown on a choke. They were all just shown on regular leads. Nobody needed a choke. But after I started winning with a choke, everyone got one. Out in the hallway at one of his first shows, I started gaiting him. And every time he'd hit the end of that lead, I'd turn him just a flip in the air and he'd come down, bark at me, wag his tail and away we'd go. Pretty soon he got to where he'd

Ch. Rebel Roc's Casanova von Kurt—"Little Daddy"—was one of America's most successful Min Pins. Many of today's top winners can be traced back to Little Daddy.

Brown

Little Daddy's first Best in Show took place in Florida. The dog, who was just eight months old, was handled by his owner, E.W. Tipton, Jr. The judge was Alva Rosenberg.

Page of New York

stay out at the end of the lead, but wouldn't hit the end. And that's when I really started winning with him."

Starting to win is exactly what Little Daddy did. At the age of eight months, under judge Alva Rosenberg, he won his first Best in Show. By the time he reached a year, he had ten Groups and five Bests to his credit. Little Daddy's show career lasted approximately four years. He was shown 162 times, won 146 Groups and 75 all-breed Bests in Show, as well as numerous breed specialties. In 1962, at the height of Little Daddy's career, he won the Quaker Oats award for Top Toy Dog, *Popular Dog*'s Top Dog Award, given to the top-winning dog in the country, and for Tipton, the Owner/Handler award. Little Daddy was shown in 28 states and Tipton said he only flew twice with the dog. Most of the traveling was done by car. Tip retired Little Daddy when the dog captured his 75th Best in Show win.

In the fall of 1986, Tipton was asked to recall some of Little Daddy's finer points:

> He was a beautiful little dog. He had a good head with good ears and dark eyes; a long neck; good rib spring; deep brisket, very short body, short in loin; a beautiful croup; fine coat with no length to it. He couldn't stand wrong. And he had a good attitude. He loved to show.
>
> I'd work with him every day and take him for walks. The neighbors would stop us and want to talk about him. Every time I'd stop to talk to the neighbors, Little Daddy would lift his leg on me. He was a mess, I tell you. He was into something all the time!
>
> He was the sweetest little dog. He always stayed with us in a motel room. He never liked the house, but he loved motels. If I'd leave, he'd go lie down in front of the door and Josie would call and call and call and Little Daddy wouldn't get up. He'd just lie there and wait for me. At a show, he was always in my arms and I never put him on the floor until I got him into the ring.

Little Daddy was seventeen years old when he died, but his legend as a top-winning show dog and sire of 34 champion get has lived on. Many of the current top breed winners have Little Daddy in their pedigrees. The Min Pin breed is fortunate that this dog and his owner, E.W. Tipton, Jr., made such a positive impact on the

A close-up of Tipton and his favorite show dog. *Alexander*

breed. Until his death in May 1987, Tipton always remained faithful to the breed that had captured his heart. Even though he went on to become one of America's few AKC licensed all-breed judges, his mind and thought never strayed far from the Miniature Pinscher.

20

Obedience

NOT ALL DOGS ARE MEANT to be conformation show dogs, nor do all owners want to participate in dog shows. All dogs, however, should have some basic obedience training if they are to be responsible housepets. The inquisitive, intelligent Min Pin is no different.

Owners wishing to learn about obedience training should contact their local kennel club and see if training classes are sponsored. If so, efforts should be made to personally communicate with the individual who is teaching the class to ascertain experience with toy dogs. Someone who has personally worked with the smaller dogs will be more understanding of their different needs and requirements than someone who does not have that background. Attending a class to see how it is run and observing the degree of control and behavior of the participants is another way to be sure of proper training techniques. A class where the dogs are running every which way, to say nothing of attacking one another, is not going to be beneficial for anyone.

There are several good obedience books available at book stores, pet shops, dog show concessionaires and from publishers that cover in detail both basic training and the more advanced requirements for dog shows. All Min Pin owners should have several of these books on their library shelves and refer to them as training progresses or a need arises. Consult the list of Howell titles at the end of this book for the range of choices.

A well-trained housepet and companion will be highly appreciated by everyone and the fun derived from working closely with the dog helps cement a closer bond of camaraderie. The Miniature Pinscher is a delight to work with and friends who come in contact with a well-trained dog will admire both the dog and its master.

Min Pins are not difficult to train, as they love the individual attention and challenge. A firm, but gentle hand, strong, yet soothing voice and the gift of love are all that is needed to blend the will of the dog with the desire of its master.

Just as there are dog shows designed to measure the conformation of one dog against first its breed standard and then its competition in the ring, there are formal obedience shows sponsored by all-breed, specialty and obedience clubs. Instructors at training classes are the best source of information regarding local events and can help guide a newcomer through the amazing world of obedience.

While conformation shows are fun, working with the Miniature Pinscher in obedience competition can be even more fulfilling. Min Pins are smart, quick to learn and give delightful performances. Obedience offers three main degrees, which are pursued by graduation steps. The first is the CD, or Companion Dog, which is followed by CDX, Companion Dog Excellent, and then UD, Utility Dog. Tracking Tests are also offered as a separate event for dogs and owners so inclined.

Anyone who wants to pursue obedience titles should not only seek assistance from local training classes but also inquire of other Min Pin owners and breeders. These individuals are usually more than happy to give advice and help to those who are trying to train the Min Pin, as this is a breed that loves obedience training and enjoys participating in competition. Many breeders who realize this like to combine conformation experience with the exploration of obedience classes and titles. Al and Dee Stutts, Der Stutz Min Pins in Arizona, are a husband and wife team who appreciate working

182

Dee Stutts takes Ch. Harper's Kopper Baron, CDX, over the high jump.

Baron also likes to leap across the broad jump.

A well-trained Canadian dog sits
by himself, waiting for his
owner, Mary Bates, Devileen
Kennels.

Al Stutts looks down at Kermit just before they
start an exercise.

Dee Stutts and her Min Pin, Ch. Der Stutz Kris
Kringle, CD.

with their Min Pins on all levels. They offer these suggestions for anyone considering obedience for the Min Pin:

The Miniature Pinscher in an obedience trial immediately attracts his audience. Happiness abounds as he quickly completes each event, seeking his master's approval and praise.

The obedience ring gives this little dog his greatest opportunity to carry on with showmanship.

Communication is the key to all dog obedience training. Owners of the Miniature Pinscher should first determine through the best books and training instructors available what things they wish to teach their great companion and then work as a unit toward achieving those goals.

As the best methods and techniques are discovered and mastered, the Min Pin and his owner will walk into the ring as a proud, happy and energetic couple.

21

The Min Pin Pet

A MINIATURE PINSCHER DOES NOT need to be a show dog to be loved. He cares not for ribbons and titles; instead, he wants companionship and attention. He delights in doing things and being busy. Whether this is going for walks, exploring new objects, attending classes and even participating in dog shows matters little to him as long as the time involved is spent with his owner. A Min Pin is a "people" dog—he relates to those around him and responds to the affection and comfort offered.

The Min Pin is the smaller, housepet variety of a breed that originally existed as a ratter. His prime purpose today is not to kill rats but to provide company and love for those who share his home.

One of the most poignant, but sad, stories that have been printed in recent years that describe the loving bond between a Min Pin and his master was written by Ernst Hartmann, of West Germany, for a 1982 issue of the German Pinscher-Schnauzer Klub's magazine. This is a true story and dates in the year 1924, when Hartmann was a 14-year-old boy who quickly became a man:

My Friend Tell

My wonderful, unforgettable little friend "Tell" was an oversized Miniature Pinscher, never cropped, black with rust-red markings. During a very difficult period in my life—a period in which I was suddenly forced to question the meaning of life—Tell was my best, ever-loyal, understanding friend. After 18 years of close companionship, I love my dearly loved Tell forever, in a pitiful, horrible way. Even today, after 57 years, I remember him as if he were right here beside me, and tears fill my eyes.

A few days before my fourteenth birthday in July 1924 and shortly before my church confirmation, the master shipwright, a friend of my family, Heinrich Weise of Frohse near the North Sea, gave me a little six-week-old Miniature Pinscher pup that I took along with me as a cabin boy on board a huge 1,000 ton river boat, which traversed the Elbe River of Northern Germany. This gigantic boat was navigated and managed by my stepfather.

I am a descendant of an old ship-building family that lived in Schoenebeck (not far from Magdeburg in East Germany), and I was impatiently awaiting the day my employment would begin. At last the big day arrived. Our river boat was docked at that time in Hamburg. At the ship-building yard owned by Weise of Frohse, a small hand-navigated boat had been built to accompany our huge river boat. I was given instructions to navigate it to Hamburg. It was to be towed by a larger boat transporting salt to that city. The navigator was a good friend of my family and he let me and my pup sleep at night in a tiny room on his boat.

Two weeks after my church confirmation, I boarded my stepfather's friend's river boat and went to work. I was still only 13 years old. I knew I could not ride along on the river boat free of charge, so I tried to make myself as useful as possible from early morning until late in the evening.

I was already well-acquainted with life on board a river boat, but everything was strange and new for my newly weaned pup Tell. He was now nine weeks old, fearless, distrustful of all others—only attached and devoted to me. He had quickly comprehended that his world as a newborn pup lying against the side of a river boat was now over.

Tell had an inborn instinct for cleanliness. Right after he was weaned, I always watched him and whenever he needed to relieve himself, I led him to a suitable place. He learned immediately and never caused me a minute's trouble. At night, we snuggled up close together on the sack filled with straw. Tell trusted me and loved me with all his heart. When we arrived in Hamburg on the fifth day of our trip, Tell was already adjusted and used to the boat. He liked being able to play and romp around, free and easy, on the river boat.

We anchored in Hamburg, and from there my stepfather picked up his new hand-paddled boat, me and, of course, Tell. We paddled to our own river boat, which was docked at the south end of Elbe Tunnel.

On my stepfather's boat, from the first day on, a very difficult period began for me. Although I was much too small for my age, very thin and frail, my hard-hearted stepfather forced me to load and unload heavy freight every day from early morning to late afternoon. Somehow, I managed to bear the physical exertion, but his brutality and crudity were sheer mental torture to me, as sensitive as I was. My little Tell helped me get over my constant depression. As if he knew how I felt, he would cuddle up to me. When he looked at me with his beautiful little dark, almond shaped eyes, I felt joy again in my heart. We grew so very attached to each other.

I was permitted to build for Tell a sturdy, water-repellent dog crate. During the fall, I padded it with freshly clipped sheep wool. Then I nailed in front of the arched entrance a curtain made of heavy canvas, with a small, vertical slit down the middle. Inside, Tell could sit, warm and dry all day long. This easily cleaned dog crate was placed up on the quarterdeck.

At first, I slept in a tiny room below the navigator's cabin and took Tell to bed with me there. But the navigator did not like that, so Tell had to sleep in his crate.

During the summer, I was often able to jump into the river from the boat and do some swimming. Attentively, Tell always watched me. One day I yelled, "Come, Tell!" Bravely, he jumped into the water from a seven-foot height and swam to me. I taught him to swim right beside me. Whenever I climbed the ladder to get back on board, Tell sat on my shoulder like a little monkey.

He learned very quickly and easily, especially, for example, that he would be rewarded if he brought me his empty bowl at lunch time. Occasionally, from the boat, I was able to catch a few fish which I put into a big keg, half-filled with water, on the quarterdeck. Tell was unbelievably adept at plunging his head under water and snapping the fish. One day, a cat jumped into our boat from a neighboring barge. The cat also wanted to catch one of our fish. Tell jumped at the cat, which fell into the water between our boat and the barge. I did not see this happen. Suddenly, Tell ran up to me, barking excitedly. Then he ran back again to the rear of the boat, then back to me. He repeated this several times. I followed him and saw the cat in the river. Thus, I was able to save the cat, which was drifting in the water and wailing like a small child. Tell, fascinated, watched all this very carefully.

Whenever we loaded up goods in sacks, Tell always wanted to go with me into the cargo rooms on the river boat. There he would always catch the scent of rats, his archenemies by instinct. Once we were unloading sacks of copra and coconuts. The sacks were being carried by Czech workers on their backs from the boat to the shore. The navigator and I had to help lift the sacks. When only a few sacks remained in the cargo room, Tell ferreted out a rat, which immediately sought cover under some sacks still lying in the corner. The workers developed hunting fever then! Quickly, they restacked 20–30 sacks, until they caught sight of the rat again. Although Tell had never caught a rat, he stood there, poised, ready to pounce at the rat. But the rat caught Tell by surprise, jumped at Tell and clenched its teeth into Tell's muzzle. Tell, however, correctly reacted like lightning: with a powerful jerk, he shook the rat from his muzzle and before the rat could get back on its legs, Tell had already grabbed it and broken its back with a firm, swift bite and jerk. From that day on, Tell was a perfect rat-catcher.

Tell was a quiet, peaceful dog, who was a very keen observer. My friends were also his friends. But woe betide the friend who—even as a playful joke—took hold of me. Tell stood there immediately, ready to jump up and bite him. At my command, he would have definitely attacked.

From the very beginning, he never left the boat unless we let him or told him to do so. If I went on shore over the plank foot bridge, he would sit down on the end of it and wait patiently until I returned. As soon as I approached the boat and yelled, "Tell, come!" he would dash toward me and, so glad to be with me again, would almost knock me down! He behaved and obeyed perfectly. I couldn't have wished for a better dog. Tell was ideal, a once in a lifetime companion.

After I had gained 18 months of training on the river boat as a cabin boy, my stepfather decided that it would be a useful experience for me to travel in a smaller boat over one of the now Soviet-occupied water routes through Mark-Brandenburg (the Brandenburg Marches) leading to Berlin. I had the opportunity to do this in September 1925.

I had looked forward to the new experience. But gloom was cast over this anticipation by my not being able to take Tell along with me. He had to remain on the river boat with my stepfather.

However, I never suspected that anything bad would happen. I knew that Tell felt at home on the boat and also thought that my stepfather would take good care of him. I didn't know that a dog can become ill and die when separated for a long period of time from the person to whom he is closely attached.

The new boat on which I now worked first took a trip to Berlin.

On the return trip to Hamburg, we met my stepfather's river boat, and passed it at approximately the speed of 6–7 knots per hour and at about 25 yards distance between us. I had run to the front of the boat and yelled loudly, "Tell!" He came out of his crate on the quarterdeck and ran toward me, up to the very rim of the boat. We ran beside each other for about a boat's length. Then I slowly lost sight of him. I would only have had to yell, "Tell, come!" and he would have jumped into the Elbe River and swum to reach me. But I was not allowed to call him.

This was the last time I ever saw my Tell. When, many weeks later, I had the opportunity to return to my stepfather's river boat, Tell was not there to meet me. My stepfather said, "After you had left, the dog got sick. I watched him a few days, but as soon as I could tell he was no longer in his right mind, I drowned him."

My dearly loved little friend Tell died pitifully, because I had left and forsaken him. He was so devotedly attached to me that he could only die without me. And I?

A Min Pin is a king and he is not about to let anyone forget it!

BIBLIOGRAPHY

ALL OWNERS of pure-bred dogs will benefit themselves and their dogs by enriching their knowledge of breeds and of canine care, training, breeding, psychology and other important aspects of dog management. The following list of books covers further reading recommended by judges, veterinarians, breeders, trainers and other authorities. Books may be obtained at the finer book stores and pet shops, or through Howell Book House Inc., publishers, New York.

BREED BOOKS

AFGHAN HOUND, Complete	Miller & Gilbert
AIREDALE, New Complete	Edwards
AKITA, Complete	Linderman & Funk
ALASKAN MALAMUTE, Complete	Riddle & Seeley
BASSET HOUND, New Complete	Braun
BLOODHOUND, Complete	Brey & Reed
BOXER, Complete	Denlinger
BRITTANY SPANIEL, Complete	Riddle
BULLDOG, New Complete	Hanes
BULL TERRIER, New Complete	Eberhard
CAIRN TERRIER, New Complete	Marvin
CHESAPEAKE BAY RETRIEVER, Complete	Cherry
CHIHUAHUA, Complete	Noted Authorities
COCKER SPANIEL, New	Kraeuchi
COLLIE, New	Official Publication of the Collie Club of America
DACHSHUND, The New	Meistrell
DALMATIAN, The	Treen
DOBERMAN PINSCHER, New	Walker
ENGLISH SETTER, New Complete	Tuck, Howell & Graef
ENGLISH SPRINGER SPANIEL, New	Goodall & Gasow
FOX TERRIER, New	Nedell
GERMAN SHEPHERD DOG, New Complete	Bennett
GERMAN SHORTHAIRED POINTER, New	Maxwell
GOLDEN RETRIEVER, New Complete	Fischer
GORDON SETTER, Complete	Look
GREAT DANE, Complete	Noted Authorities
GREAT DANE, The—Dogdom's Apollo	Draper
GREAT PYRENEES, Complete	Strang & Giffin
IRISH SETTER, New Complete	Eldredge & Vanacore
IRISH WOLFHOUND, Complete	Starbuck
JACK RUSSELL TERRIER, Complete	Plummer
KEESHOND, New Complete	Cash
LABRADOR RETRIEVER, New Complete	Warwick
LHASA APSO, Complete	Herbel
MALTESE, Complete	Cutillo
MASTIFF, History and Management of the	Baxter & Hoffman
MINIATURE SCHNAUZER, New	Kiedrowski
NEWFOUNDLAND, New Complete	Chern
NORWEGIAN ELKHOUND, New Complete	Wallo
OLD ENGLISH SHEEPDOG, Complete	Mandeville
PEKINGESE, Quigley Book of	Quigley
PEMBROKE WELSH CORGI, Complete	Sargent & Harper
POODLE, New	Irick
POODLE CLIPPING AND GROOMING BOOK, Complete	Kalstone
PORTUGUESE WATER DOG, Complete	Braund & Miller
ROTTWEILER, Complete	Freeman
SAMOYED, New Complete	Ward
SCOTTISH TERRIER, New Complete	Marvin
SHETLAND SHEEPDOG, The New	Riddle
SHIH TZU, Joy of Owning	Seranne
SHIH TZU, The (English)	Dadds
SIBERIAN HUSKY, Complete	Demidoff
TERRIERS, The Book of All	Marvin
WEIMARANER, Guide to the	Burgoin
WEST HIGHLAND WHITE TERRIER, Complete	Marvin
WHIPPET, Complete	Pegram
YORKSHIRE TERRIER, Complete	Gordon & Bennett

BREEDING

ART OF BREEDING BETTER DOGS, New	Onstott
BREEDING YOUR OWN SHOW DOG	Seranne
HOW TO BREED DOGS	Whitney
HOW PUPPIES ARE BORN	Prine
INHERITANCE OF COAT COLOR IN DOGS	Little

CARE AND TRAINING

BEYOND BASIC DOG TRAINING	Bauman
COUNSELING DOG OWNERS, Evans Guide for	Evans
DOG OBEDIENCE, Complete Book of	Saunders
NOVICE, OPEN AND UTILITY COURSES	Saunders
DOG CARE AND TRAINING FOR BOYS AND GIRLS	Saunders
DOG NUTRITION, Collins Guide to	Collins
DOG TRAINING FOR KIDS	Benjamin
DOG TRAINING, Koehler Method of	Koehler
DOG TRAINING Made Easy	Tucker
GO FIND! Training Your Dog to Track	Davis
GROOMING DOGS FOR PROFIT	Gold
GUARD DOG TRAINING, Koehler Method of	Koehler
MOTHER KNOWS BEST—The Natural Way to Train Your Dog	Benjamin
OPEN OBEDIENCE FOR RING, HOME AND FIELD, Koehler Method of	Koehler
STONE GUIDE TO DOG GROOMING FOR ALL BREEDS	Stone
SUCCESSFUL DOG TRAINING, The Pearsall Guide to	Pearsall
TEACHING DOG OBEDIENCE CLASSES—Manual for Instructors	Volhard & Fisher
TOY DOGS, Kalstone Guide to Grooming All	Kalstone
TRAINING THE RETRIEVER	Kersley
TRAINING TRACKING DOGS, Koehler Method of	Koehler
TRAINING YOUR DOG—Step by Step Manual	Volhard & Fisher
TRAINING YOUR DOG TO WIN OBEDIENCE TITLES	Morsell
TRAIN YOUR OWN GUN DOG, How to	Goodall
UTILITY DOG TRAINING, Koehler Method of	Koehler
VETERINARY HANDBOOK, Dog Owner's Home	Carlson & Giffin

GENERAL

A DOG'S LIFE	Burton & Allaby
AMERICAN KENNEL CLUB 1884-1984—A Source Book	American Kennel Club
CANINE TERMINOLOGY	Spira
COMPLETE DOG BOOK, The	Official Publication of American Kennel Club
DOG IN ACTION, The	Lyon
DOG BEHAVIOR, New Knowledge of	Pfaffenberger
DOG JUDGE'S HANDBOOK	Tietjen
DOG PSYCHOLOGY	Whitney
DOGSTEPS, The New	Elliott
DOG TRICKS	Haggerty & Benjamin
EYES THAT LEAD—Story of Guide Dogs for the Blind	Tucker
FRIEND TO FRIEND—Dogs That Help Mankind	Schwartz
FROM RICHES TO BITCHES	Shattuck
HAPPY DOG/HAPPY OWNER	Siegal
IN STITCHES OVER BITCHES	Shattuck
JUNIOR SHOWMANSHIP HANDBOOK	Brown & Mason
OUR PUPPY'S BABY BOOK (blue or pink)	
SUCCESSFUL DOG SHOWING, Forsyth Guide to	Forsyth
WHY DOES YOUR DOG DO THAT?	Bergman
WILD DOGS in Life and Legend	Riddle
WORLD OF SLED DOGS, From Siberia to Sport Racing	Coppinger